NON-STOP LOVE

A Journey Towards Joy

Michelle S. Kim

A Korean-American immigrant's
personal story of freedom, from cultural shame
to everlasting joy in Christ.

Non-Stop Love: A Journey Towards Joy
Trilogy Christian Publishers A Wholly Owned Subsidary of Trinity Broadcasting Network
2442 Michelle Drive Tustin, CA 92780

Rights Department, 2442 Michelle Drive, Tustin, CA 92780.
Trilogy Christian Publishing/TBN and colophon are trademarks of Trinit Broadcasting Network.
Cover design by: the Trilogy design team with the photograph of Gary Krzywicki.
For information about special discounts for bulk purchases, please conta Trilogy Christian Publishing.
Trilogy Disclaimer: The views and content expressed in this book are those of the author and may not necessarily reflect the views and doctrin of Trilogy Christian Publishing or the Trinity Broadcasting Network.
Manufactured in the United States of America
10 9 8 7 6 5 4 3 2 1
Library of Congress Cataloging-in-Publication Data is available.
ISBN: 978-1-63769-936-2
E-ISBN: 978-1-63769-937-9

Dear Richard and Ashley,

You two are the most precious God-given blessings for me and Dad! I love you both more than anything in the whole wide world! I'm so proud of you two! As you already know, I have no treasures other than you two, and I have no wealth to pass on except for faith in Jesus. All I want to ask of you is one thing: to keep your faith in Jesus as your Savior and to walk with Him for all of your lives and give Him love and honor.

Acknowledgment

This book is the product of the endeavor by a special God-given team.

First of all, I'd like to honor and thank Roxanne Breitenfeld as the finalist for my book. She came through after years of prayer and was the perfect, hand-picked editor by God, having a master's in middle and secondary education and serving as a high school English teacher.

Second, I thank my daughter, Ashley E. Kim, who majored in Linguistics and is a Phi Beta Kappa scholar. The level of writing in my book could not have been possible without her commitment and dedication. I'm especially thankful for her devotion to her mother, which persisted during major transitions of her life with her first full-time job and marriage.

I also thank the people God placed in my life, who helped me in various stages of need: Pat Salinowicz, who endured my bad phraseology. She published her first children's book and became an author the year before. Jonathan Hong, who I consider family. Gary Krzywicki, who blessed me with his magnificent photography for my book cover. All of his photographs point to the Creator, who is the best artist of the whole universe. Richard Y. Kim, a man of technology. He always has my back and helps me anytime I need him. He is needed greatly, endlessly, for his mom is technologically challenged. I thank you all from the bottom of my heart and pray for you for God's extra blessings!

Also, I thank so many of my friends for their prayers! Without their prayers, I cannot imagine that this would have been possible. I'm so grateful for their sincere prayers for me and this book! And I thank God eternally, who answers our prayers and makes all things possible!

Contents

Preface 9

My Grandmother 13

   1. Revealing My Shameful Existence. 13

   2. Errands for My Grandmother 17

   3. A Witch 21

   4. A Journey to Forgiveness 36

   5. Non-Stop Love 48

My Father 61

   1. My Mom's Lie 61

   2. My School Experiences 66

   3. A Culture of Shame. 75

   4. My Lies. 85

   5. The Gift of God. 90

My Mom & I 103

   1. My Mom's Young Daughter 103

   2. A Pledge with The Prince of Egypt. 108

   3. A New Trial. 113

   4. Seasons of Struggles. 131

   5. God-Given Discernment. 161

6. God's Perfect Plan for My Mom and Me 166

His Rod & Staff. **173**

1. My Born-Again Experience 174

2. My Very First Holy Spirit Encounter 189

3. Breaking Free from Chains and Bondage. 198

4. The Word of God that Raised Me 208

5. My Hands and Miracles 216

The Most Extraordinary Season of My Life. **237**

1. A Voyage to My Home Church. 238

2. Excitement Even Without Good News 246

3. Divine Appointment 255

4. The Trip to Korea 264

5. How He Encourages Me. 280

Afterword. **293**

Preface

Growing up in South Korea, I had some friends at school who didn't like their names. I later found out that a few of them had paid money to change their legal names.

However, they didn't hate their family names like I did. They proudly followed the tradition of carrying their father's last name. Unlike them, my last name was the same as my mom's. As a fatherless child, I had no choice. So I endured people's judgmental, disapproving looks whenever they recognized that I carried my mom's last name. It made me feel vulnerable.

When I came to America, I discovered that most married women changed their last names to their husbands'. It was the norm, the standard to do so. This tradition was the rescue I needed from my traumatic past.

Unlike most other Korean women who immigrated to America and kept their maiden names with pride, I adopted my husband's last name immediately. Then my husband and I started to work out a new American name for me, as we had done for our precious children.

In 1999, I received citizenship here in America and achieved my new legal name, Michelle S. Kim. It was a relief for me at the time, but it was also before I found out that my biological father's last name is the same.

In 2000, I was "born-again," and it was a turning

point in my life. But despite this, I felt a little confused about my name. As a female Korean immigrant, I realized that no other married Korean women that I knew had changed their names like I did.

In my prayers, I asked God what He thought about my name, and He revealed what He thought of it: it's a new identity. In the Bible, God gave Abram and Jacob new names, Abraham and Israel, and transformed Saul into the Apostle Paul.

Although I am far from them, I am also no longer who I was. Through my book, I hope my readers will see the dramatic process of how I was transformed from a troubled pessimist to a renewed optimist.

Some might say that my story doesn't contain any remarkable successes, but rather than tangible successes, it is about my human and inner struggles in my relationships. I had emotional, spiritual, and cultural chains binding me for decades while also being challenged by my own family and their troubles. This is my victory story of being set free from these chains, from the shame and condemnation of Confucian culture, and the lies that I had been bound to, all within the realm of spiritual warfare that we cannot see.

My trials are ongoing, but I rejoice because I have learned that God works in all things for my good (Romans 8:28), so I am victorious in Him (John 16:33, 1 John 5:4). Without my trials, I could never have learned patience, character, and hope (Romans 5:3–5), which enriched my life.

It was God who pressed me on with encouragement to share with others about the peace and joy that I have found, which is granted by Him and has been kept within me. Surely, I couldn't hold it in me anymore (Luke 19:40).

Although I am less than the least of all the Lord's people, this grace was given me: to preach to the Gentiles the boundless riches of Christ, and to make plain to everyone the administration of this mystery, which for ages past was kept hidden in God, who created all things.

Ephesians 3:8–9

Even to me, such a sinner, God gave the honor of being saved and carrying the gospel to everyone because He loves all and wants to save all and desires for none to perish, including both Israelites and Gentiles!

I hope and pray for my readers who will read my story that the same God who met me meets you with unfailing love and bathes you in it so that you can find the joy that I have found and be saturated in it!

But God chose the foolish things of the world to shame the wise; God chose the weak things of the world to shame the strong. God chose the lowly things of this world and the despised things—and the things that are not—to nullify the things that are, so that no one may boast before him.

1 Corinthians 1:27–29

And I thank Pastor Kenny Hong for his preaching that awoke my soul and led me to my true salvation through this page. I pray that God will bless him and his family and church abundantly and eternally.

In Christ,

Michelle S. Kim.

My Grandmother

Instead of your shame you will receive a double portion, and instead of disgrace you will rejoice in your inheritance; and so you will inherit a double portion in your land, and everlasting joy will be yours.

Isaiah 61:7

1. Revealing My Shameful Existence

I was born and raised in Korea in my grandmother's house in the late '60s to the late '80s. My earliest memory of that time was when I was about five years old. It's a scene in my mind of my grandmother and mother talking at bedtime one night. My grandmother was angrily talking to my mom, and what she said horrified me, sticking with me for years, until my thirties when I was "born-again" in Christ. Though I grew up there, I don't have any memories related to my grandmother prior to that night.

That first memory of my grandmother was around the same time my grandfather had seemingly disappeared without a trace. It must have been the same year he passed away from a startling stroke. Nobody explained to me what had happened to my grandfather, even through his funeral, which I didn't even know was a funeral. His picture was propped up on a table with food, laced with a black ribbon. Guests poured into our house and bowed down to his picture one by one. I know I stopped seeing him after this event, and after a while, I guessed that I wouldn't see him anymore.

I recall vaguely — more than a couple of times — he came home drunk, calling my name at the front door with a sweet ripe persimmon in his hand. He would feed it to me while I sat on his lap. He had been the only one who had adored me in the house, and that expressive affection had lasted for such a short time before it was gone.

Back to the scene that night: hearing my grandmother's voice stressed me. I pretended to be asleep, pulling the comforter over my face. When I heard my grandmother talk about me hysterically, sitting right next to me, I felt wide awake, and my heart thumped loudly.

We all slept in the same bedroom, with at least two or more aunts — my mom's younger sisters — each given a Korean futon, a thick padded spread, and a comforter, on top of a heated floor covered by vinyl. In older Korean houses, there is a furnace outside, under every bedroom's cement flooring. The furnace is heated with coal, which heats up the stone flooring to provide warmth.

My grandmother was extremely thrifty, so she limited heating to only one room. In the winter, we would live more closely and sleep in one bedroom together to keep warm.

Every night, we would wipe the bedroom floor, then set up the futons, which were folded away in the closet in the morning. Wiping the bedroom floor became my nightly chore. There was no space to walk around in the room after our futons were set up for bedtime.

Grandmother continued rebuking my mom in a mean and irritated way.

"You pay attention to raise this kid right! Oh, I'm so worried! How will you raise this kid?"

Why is she angry? What did I do wrong? I thought, afraid.

"You know the *horojasik* with no father, right? What a shame! You make sure this fatherless child doesn't bring more shame from the people out there pointing fingers at you and me. She's already shameful; make sure she doesn't bring more shame," Grandmother kept muttering with bitter sighs.

I didn't fully understand it, but it sounded horrible. The word *horojasik* overflowed with a feeling of shame even to a child who had never heard it before. I gathered hints of its meaning from what my grandmother said. *It's related to my father. I have no father, which must be terrible. Grandmother feels disgusted at it. People out there will find it out and point their fingers at me and mom, and it's humiliating.*

Horojasik is a child without a father. The word is full of contempt and derision. It made me swallow hard. I had never heard the word before, and I had no idea why it was shameful. But I knew I was the shame.

At the same time, I could imagine people staring and laughing at me. I closed my eyes tightly to try to erase the picture from my mind. The feeling of shame attacked me, mortifying and embarrassing all at once. It felt like a punch to my stomach, a bomb that burned me down instantly, marking me with an unbearable shame that I felt like I could never face. Nobody, not even my mom, knew how I was trembling at the shame under the comforter that night. *That is me, my secret, my label, that nobody can ever find out.* It pierced my heart.

I wished I could disappear in that moment. Covering my face with the comforter, I wanted to bury the shame someplace deep. But the shame was pulling me down even deeper to bury me. I had nowhere to go. Buried under the shame and feeling choked, I clenched my teeth, trying to endure it.

Then, I started to feel something completely new that I had never felt before. Bitterness and anger started to rise up from the darkness that I felt, somehow giving me courage and lifting me up.

I fell asleep feeling determined that I would never, ever bring shame unto my mom, that I would rather die than to do so, and that I would prove my grandmother wrong. I hated my grandmother for revealing my shame.

2. Errands for My Grandmother

Periodically, my grandmother would order me to go get her *makkoli*, a sweet Korean rice wine. The first time was when I started elementary school; she walked me to the brewery to show me where to get it. Then when she called me and commanded it, I had to go immediately, carrying a two-liter yellow bronze tea kettle, walking for about half an hour.

Every time, I walked in frustration with the unwieldy kettle. Coming home was not easy. I had to take care not to spill any of the *makkoli* out of the heavy kettle, but above that, I was afraid to go home.

Nobody cared how heavy my burden was carrying out this duty. There was fear and anxiety related to the consequence of that drink. I was ashamed to be the one to bring my grandmother the liquor, knowing that in her drunkenness, she would abuse my mom. I dragged myself back home as slowly as possible.

As soon as I entered the house, she would yell at me with a burning glare, "Why did it take so long? Did you stop by somewhere?" She expected there to be absolutely no delays or excuses when it came to her orders. Whatever she demanded, whether it was day or night, rain or shine, hot or cold, from elementary school all the way up to high school, it was to be done. It was impossible to disobey or resist her, even though I hated her and her commands with my whole being. But my body was conditioned to perform her orders automatically as if it belonged to her. No matter how much I hated her orders, I had no idea how to avoid them. I was just a helpless child, following the rules in her house. Everyone and everything in the house were to do what she commanded as soon as the command came out of her mouth.

The most frequent order that I received from my grandmother was massaging her. Nobody else wanted to do it, and everyone, including my mom, looked to me as if I were the only one who could do this task. It was my duty when Grandmother hollered, "massage." Though I was never really taught how to perform a massage, I was like her personal masseuse for more than twelve years. Whenever I was called by her, I ran to her like a robot and massaged her legs and arms, almost on a daily basis for half an hour or more, until she fell asleep. There was no affection between us; it was just a chore and child labor.

Massaging her every time was agonizing for me, especially when I wanted to play or do something else. She was like my master, like an evil queen in a fairy tale. She selfishly engaged in only what she liked in her house, regardless of anyone else's opinions or preferences. I lived like her slave to please her, just for my own survival.

The other errand that I hated as much as bringing in the liquor was collecting money from people around the town. My grandmother had a private money lending business with high interest. Although she had not gone to school, she was literate and very shrewd with money.

As soon as I started high school, my grandmother assigned me to be her debt collector, as if she had been waiting for me to grow up to do so. She had me collecting from debtors in the area daily. There were several people to see, and it took a couple of hours to make a round trip.

I absolutely hated it because I felt like "the bad guy," having to do her dirty work. Each time, the debtors looked so miserable, making me feel so guilty. But over time, the debtors and I developed mutual sympathy for each other, despite being in opposite positions. We understood the consequences of not paying and not collecting.

The only times I could be off-duty from debt collecting was when I had too much homework or tests going on at school, especially in my senior year. I was an honor student, and studying or school were the only reasons that made sense to my grandmother. She had not gone to school herself, so maybe that was why she accepted those reasons.

When I brought home random certificates or awards from school, she was stunned and eyed me up and down, doubtfully. She never looked proud or happy, just disturbed, with her usual angry air. None of her children had ever brought such things home, which I later heard from my mom.

I was her errand girl 24/7, but there were some extremely rare moments that I seemed to be her granddaughter. Occasionally, my grandmother would be asked about me while we were together. She would introduce me awkwardly and proudly that I was her granddaughter, doing very well at school and bringing home prizes. She should have stopped there, but she added, very gracefully, that it was she who had raised me graciously, and she wondered out loud what good this child would bring her in return, or what worth raising this kid would be for her in the future, for all that she had done for me. And as my grandmother would finish talking and look at me, she would produce a sudden fake smile to finish her performance. I would freeze, trying my best to not reveal any expressions on my face.

3. A Witch

Part 1

I saw my grandmother as nothing but a witch to me and my mom.

The lady who lived next door owned a set of fifty books of children's fairy tales from around the world; she was kind and let me borrow them, but each time she sighed that her own children didn't read her books.

What the lady didn't know was that I was seeking a witch as bad as my own grandmother in those books. All of the fairy tales I read had a story about witches, describing what they were and how terrible they were. Only those books of fairy tales, which described all kinds of witches in the world, seemed to understand my troubles, and it comforted me.

But still, not one could describe the witch that I lived with. My grandmother beat every single witch. She surpassed all of the witches in the fairy tales I read.

Hansel and Gretel were able to get rid of the witch in their story by tricking her into the oven of her cookie house and then running away, but I had to live with my witch continuously and forever. And there were no witches that tortured their own daughters or grand-daughters.

There is a Korean saying that when someone stub-bornly refuses to listen to reason and insists that their way is right even when they are wrong, that they "insist on black for white and white for black." My grandmother was always this way.

Whoever listened to her at any given time had to give their total consent without argument or hesitation. Nobody could talk back to her even when what she was saying sounded like complete nonsense. For example, she would often say things that were the opposite of what I learned in school: old people have to eat better than children, and children do not have to eat well. If there was a special dish on the table, we dared not touch it until she tasted it and finished her portion, and then we could eat her leftovers. She never failed to comment that that was a blessing for us.

And whether she was drunk or sober, we had no option but to say "yes" quickly and firmly when she asked anything. Our facial expressions and attitudes had to be perfectly agreeable to her eyes and pleasing to her ears. Sometimes, my aunts, mom, and I became anxious in the midst of our private conversations, worrying if she heard us with her sharp hearing. If she did, she would suddenly show up, terrifying us, asking, "What did you say?" frowning or examining us, "You didn't like what I said?" as if already provoked, not to miss any details. Then we had to act really well and lie with absolute certainty, "No, of course not!" If she saw or heard anyone irritated by her demands even slightly, they were dead on that day. It was a dreadful moment when she asked, "Why did you frown?" Even if we denied it, she would cry out, "Yes, you did. You surely did! You may be able to deceive other people, but nobody deceives me!" My grandmother's word was the law in our house, and it had to be effective at the cost of our freedom because nobody could deal with her deadly temper.

Even outside of her house, she looked for people to devour. It didn't matter if it was an open market or the middle of the street or if she was surrounded by crowds. Regardless of right or wrong, whoever was in her way could be caught by her. She started fights, grabbing onto her victim's hair so they couldn't escape and then beating them. She never let go of her opponent even when they yielded to her; they would have to bow down until she was satisfied. She never lost such fights that she started, and nobody in town dared to oppose her.

Every once in a while, she would drink with her sons-in-law, my uncles-in-law, one at a time. It seemed like a game to her: she would pick small fights with them just to clash and trample her victims. She humiliated them one by one. My uncles-in-law were aghast, to be defeated by a ferocious woman intoxicated with alcohol. It was interesting to observe their reactions and humiliation. Yet, their experience was only a quarter of the savagery that my mom received.

They would confide in me that, after one or two experiences like that with her, they couldn't overcome the blow to their pride by Grandmother. I was surprised by their honesty, that they would confide such a thing to their niece, but it also gave me some solace, knowing that I wasn't abnormal or the only one who was sick and tired of Grandmother's drunkenness and craziness. At the same time, I wondered how they could say that when they knew I lived with her. Probably, they could never believe or imagine how she hurt her own sick child and her granddaughter. Nobody had seen how she abused and destroyed us with their own eyes.

Part 2

When my grandmother started drinking, she would pick a fight with anyone around for any reason, which was unbearable. Everyone in the house would hide, but she would always summon my mom to go over her accumulated charges like it was a trial. She would begin with an angry interrogation, which would erupt into rage, condemnation, nonsensical blaming, repeated rebuking, horrifying misjudgment, and bringing forth every single thing she disliked or felt irritated by about my mom. It was an ugly display of her own desolate self-pity, misery, and self-vindication.

During this trial, she tried to provoke my mom cruelly, never expressing any love for her as a mother, but making comments on her attitude and facial expressions. My mom knelt before her like a criminal, bowing her head down and saying nothing. Sometimes she cried out, "That's wrong!" or "I didn't do that!" but mostly agreeing, "I am guilty of that" and "I'm sorry." But her apologies never satisfied my grandmother.

Sooner or later, my grandmother would transform horrifically like the Hulk, triggered by blowing rage. There was no way of stopping it as she drank more. Her outbursts of screaming and howling were like a beast. As if she couldn't hold back any longer, she would forcefully act out by slapping my mom's cheeks so haughtily, even laughing to release the tension from her body, and grabbing my mom by her hair and shaking her head like a toy.

She spat on her again and again, pouring out her stress and wrath on her tiniest, weakest, handicapped child, as if this one had ruined her whole life. It was so monstrous to observe this real-life horror movie as a child, but it happened right in front of my eyes. The worst part of this chaos to me was that I could not rescue my mom from that real-life devil, only being able to watch like it was a movie.

My grandmother was aware that I was close to them, exposed to see the whole thing, and she heard my devastated crying and wailing, but she never heeded my crying. I wondered if she did it so severely just for me to witness it. I hid myself behind a small piece of furniture, trying to conceal my tears and my terror, especially when I was so young. I was faint with horror, choking on my own tears and thinking I would die. It was beyond what a child could bear. Nobody helped my mom. Nobody cared about me. All of my aunts disappeared, hiding from their own mother's insanity. Two of my aunts left the house too soon, faraway to Seoul, and one helpless aunt with a learning disability stayed behind, working as a housemaid.

I did not only cry, but I also prayed a million prayers to God with my every breath to rescue my mom. However, God never came to rescue us during that time. I was traumatized watching my mom be beaten by my grandmother. But even though God never answered, I could not stop praying. I just didn't know how to *not* pray or how to desert the last hope that I had, which was the only thing I had to hold on to.

When I was an upper elementary or middle school student, I sprinted out of the house, running to a public phone booth at the bottom of a long hill by an intersection. Although I was physically free from my grandmother's hand and out of the house, the whole world froze in my eyes. The people and cars on the street halted as I ran to the phone booth to call my aunt in Seoul and ask for her help.

She was the only one who could have helped us, but she would not come because she lived too far away. Although I could hear my aunt's voice comforting me through the phone, it echoed so faintly and hopelessly from beyond the mountains. Everything and everyone on the street were still frozen in my eyes. I heard nothing on my way back home to rescue my mom.

As I entered the house, I could hear the sound of yelling and screaming again, and I could see my grandmother vividly even before I actually saw her. The house felt completely separated and isolated like an island, containing only my monster grandmother and my poor mom, so far far away from any help from the rest of the world. But I still cried for help for hours until I lost my voice. But nobody ever came, and nobody ever helped us.

Sometimes, with tremendous courage, I protested against my grandmother to protect my mom in my childlike way. I wished I could transform into a heroic rescuer, jumping in front of my mom to protect her. In reality, I crawled up next to my mom, kneeling together with her and begging for Grandmother's forgiveness, rubbing my hands frantically. Grandmother never cared. She would continue howling like a beast and beating my mom like a monster. She looked like a devil in my mind. Her body would shake maniacally as she beat my mom.

At the same time, her mouth pumped out all kinds of curses and profanity. With her tongue alone, she could slaughter both of us more than a million times. Her words cut me into pieces, blowing me away like dust. My mom and I were parasites to her, worse than all other people. We were even less valuable than bugs, completely useless to her. She shouted that we were killing her, we were choking her to death. My mom was the most worthless of all the worthless. She never should have been born. She should have died. "Die! Die! Die! Disappear! Go away with your child right now!" She kept asking my mom over and over again why she was born and why she was tormenting her mother.

Her screaming was fully saturated with the worst, stomach-churning curses. I have never heard anyone use more foul language than my grandmother in my whole life. It disgusted me and made me feel nauseous. I felt like all of the curses from my grandmother tore me down to my soul, but they also pulled me from fear to wrath to a higher degree of internal rage. It tempted me, making me want to die like a suicide bomber, taking her down with me. The feeling grew as I got older.

I wish I had no ears to hear her curses which provoked me. She kept screaming at the top of her lungs at my mom to get out of her house with her worthless child immediately. She was not a grandmother to me, only a witch.

Through it all, my mom never resisted her. She yielded her body like a lifeless mannequin. My grandmother was twice the size of my tiny mom and the tallest and biggest amongst the entire household. Even after I finished growing in high school, she was still bigger, taller, and much stronger than me.

At the end of my grandmother's cruel and insane show of inebriety, she would drag my mom like baggage out of the living room into the courtyard. Then she would start throwing out all of our belongings — our bedding, clothes, blankets, pillows; everything was thrown out of the house, and then she would lock the door.

My mom and I were instantly homeless right in front of our grandmother's house. If we were lucky, this only happened once a month. Sometimes this happened every week. It happened so randomly I could never be prepared. I just suffered, unable to build any immunity against her violence.

We would stand for hours at the door. I kept my back towards the street so that nobody could recognize me. I was mortified at the thought of any acquaintances passing by and seeing me. Thankfully, the house was located behind a huge church near the end of a long hill that was at the border of another district, so it wasn't a busy street. Also, my mom had sent me to a school in a different district, so I didn't have many classmates in the area.

We had to wait until Grandmother fell asleep for my aunt to open the door for us. Sometimes we waited for hours until dark. My mom went in quickly, but I hesitated, hating to go into the same house again. The worst part was having to sleep in the same room with my grandmother after everything that happened.

I slept on the farthest end away from Grandmother. Once I started middle school, my mom and I started using another small room. I insisted to my mom that we stay in that room even in the winter. It was possible with an electric blanket under the bedding. I wore a coat and mittens to do my homework, but I didn't care as long as I didn't have to see my grandmother. Mom paid extra to Grandmother for the electricity bill.

Even when Grandmother wasn't drunk, there was still a hostile atmosphere in the house. A day that did not bring anger to her was a lucky day. Everyone in the house wanted to keep it peaceful and tiptoed in her presence.

My grandmother was a landlord, renting out units with a couple of kitchens and a shared bathroom to three families. The other tenants across the courtyard behaved well and communicated sympathetically with us. Grandmother was like an evil tyrant. We felt relieved when she went out and enjoyed temporary relief if she went away overnight. I jumped with freedom, and it felt like a party without her.

Part 3

Grandmother, my mom, and I attended the Catholic church that was on the other side of our house regularly. I went at a different hour, but every Sunday, I saw her dressed in her best outfit and makeup which she did only for church and special occasions.

She looked both ridiculous and scary to me. She knew how to act modestly and humbly for her own benefit, especially in front of the priest, anyone with authority, or the very rich.

To my amazement, the priest visited my grandmother and drank alcohol with her at least once or twice. It was an unbelievable, jaw-dropping scene that my grandmother did not allow herself to become insane with him. She was attentive, displaying perfect decorum. That was the only exception to my grandmother's insanity. My mom doesn't remember it at all. There are some things that she doesn't recall, perhaps because of her trauma.

As soon as she came back home from church, if there were children playing near the front of the house, she would rush to grab a bucket of water from the back of the house to throw on the children. She hollered at the children who began running away, soaked and crying, "How dare you! Get away from my house!" It was one of the most disheartening things I had ever seen. I felt so humiliated and angry; I didn't want any of my acquaintances to know that she was my grandmother and that I lived in the same house as her.

Seeing her like this made me angry and want to fight her. She made me feel so worthless, being confined to her house. There was nothing I could do but to wait for this time of torture and slavery to pass. Our only goal from day to day was to survive.

There were some occasions when my mom did something specifically related to me, which provoked my grandmother to anger. These occasions were when she bought something for me. We could hide it if it was small, but when she bought me a desk to study, it was too big to hide. Grandmother became extremely angry as soon as she noticed it, as if my mom was never allowed to do anything for me. She asked, "Why does she need a desk? She can study anywhere. You can't study if you don't have a desk? Nonsense! Why do you spend money like that! You don't pay me enough for your living expenses! If you had the money for a desk, you should have paid me first!" My mom had bought me a desk two times, but we returned it the first time because Grandmother's wrath was uncontrollable. After a year or so, my mom bought me a bigger and better desk around middle school. It was my first and last piece of furniture. The second time, Grandmother was still angry, but not as badly as the first time, so we kept it. It was always like that—everything had to be consulted with and granted by Grandmother. There seemed to be nothing, no rights or freedom that my mom could have for me, even to buy things with her own money.

I grew into a pessimistic teenager, loving gloomy, rainy days and the winter. Dismal weather, with loud thunder and lightning, and the season of cold stillness comforted my hurting and sentimental soul.

To my surprise, my uncle from Seoul, my grandmother's only son, brought me a Walkman, which I treasured. I started to listen to popular American songs in my middle school years. Some days I cried under my thick comforter for hours, listening to the Bee Gees through headphones. I didn't have the freedom to cry—I risked getting caught by Grandmother. Their top song on my cassette tape was "Tragedy." I didn't understand the lyrics, but the tune was tragic, just like my heart.

Over a million times, I imagined escaping from Grandmother's house, but the conclusion was always *I can't*. Knowing that I was my mom's only hope, I couldn't run away, leaving her with no hope.

Throughout my childhood, I would occasionally ask my mom with courage if we could live somewhere other than at Grandmother's. I told my mom that I could live anywhere else, giving examples like a straw-roofed hut, the mountainside, or even in a cave, as long as it was anywhere other than there. However, my mom never heeded my begging. We had no money, and she couldn't afford a decent living by herself, even though she was always working in my eyes. She tailored and altered both Korean costumes and modern clothes from some women in the area, in the corner of the bedroom.

The question I asked her most frequently, though, was if Grandmother, who abused my mom, was truly my mom's mom or a stepmother. She always gave me the same answer, that she was her real mother. I had read tons and tons of fairy tales and stories, so that didn't make sense to me. None of those witches ever hated and tortured their own children or grandchildren—ever.

When I started high school, suicidal thoughts tempted me. I searched for all kinds of methods of dying. I was so sick and tired of hearing Grandmother's nonsense every day under the same roof. I looked for the easiest and quickest way of dying. Every sharp-edged tool drew my attention. It tempted me, whispering in my ears that I should do it instead of living like that. I wrestled with the thought.

Then one day, I felt determined after being so depressed from hours of crying. But just as I felt determined, suddenly, an image of Jesus dying on the cross flashed in my mind. Sensing His eyes on me, I couldn't do it. Betraying Him like that wasn't allowed; I felt that way from deep within me. I wept bitterly. The fear of hell haunted my guilty conscience. And, at that moment, in my valley of the shadow of death, I cried out to Jesus. Strangely, I felt an irresistible hope in my agony, and I chose not to let myself drown from all the curses that had been showered on me by Grandmother. There is a Korean proverb, "A dragon rises from a small stream." This is equivalent to the American saying "from rags to riches." But to me, it felt deeper: I wanted to prove to myself that I could be better than my situation. I prayed this proverb to help me overcome my constant battle, the overwhelming impulse to just escape. Since I chose to hope, I became more determined to tolerate my present in order to rise up in the future.

When I moved to Seoul for college, we moved into my uncle's house, which my grandmother had bought for him. She adored her only son extremely; she despised daughters. Her generation believed that a son is a blessing since he is the one who continues the family line.

In Seoul, I met and fell in love with Young, who I decided to marry, during my college years. I was only twenty-one. Nobody, not my mom, grandmother, aunt, or anyone else, opposed me marrying at such a young age and even leaving to another country. My circumstances definitely made it easy to decide to marry and leave the country. It was a blessing that I could finally leave Grandmother's house.

Ten years later, my mom arrived in America to live with me, and she told me something about my wedding gift money from back then that I didn't know about. In Korea, people gift money for special events like a wedding or funeral, just for a small gift in return. Anybody can come and donate without being invited, except for some special weddings run by invitation. The money helps directly for the occasion and needs. My wedding was free in a Catholic church after the sacrament of matrimony. And so my grandmother took most of my wedding gift money, leaving almost nothing for me. Most of the guests who came and donated had been friends and acquaintances of Grandmother, so she took most of it, charging my mom for numerous living expenses in the past. So the money my mom gave me when I left Korea was borrowed from Grandmother, not my wedding gift, which she had to pay back with interest for years.

Also, on the day I finally left the house, immediately after I left for the airport to go to America, my grandmother commanded my mom, who had just sent her only child far, far away, to immediately empty the room that we had shared. So she emptied it and moved to the smallest room in the house.

When you pass through the waters, I will be with you; and when you pass through the rivers, they will not sweep over you. When you walk through the fire, you will not be burned; the flames will not set you ablaze.

Isaiah 43:2

4. A Journey to Forgiveness

I grew up in Mokpo, a small harbor city located in the southwestern end of Korea. It was a quiet city where not much happened. Although it wasn't small enough for everyone to know everyone, it was small enough that when something interesting happened, people reacted, rather than just passing by quickly like in a larger city.

When I was in fifth grade, my youngest aunt was a senior in high school. One day, I noticed she was reading something in a different language. It drew my attention and mesmerized me. When I asked her what she was studying, she told me it was English. It sounded so mysterious and magical to me. That was when I first discovered the English language.

I asked her how I could learn it, and she told me I would have to wait until seventh grade, which is the first year of middle school in Korea. I couldn't believe that I would have to wait two more years. So I couldn't wait to go to middle school, only because I wanted to learn English so badly.

Due to an illness in her early years, my mom was handicapped and had not gone to middle school or even graduated from elementary school. So nobody in my grandmother's house paid attention to what I wished or dreamed for. I had wanted to learn to play the piano, but we didn't have a piano or money.

There was a college graduate who tutored piano and English in her home. During winter vacation, which lasted two months, from the end of December to the beginning of February, right before elementary school graduation, I told her that I wanted to learn English. She made me an offer that if I brought ten friends who also wanted to study English, she would teach me for free. Luckily, I was able to gather seven students who wanted to get a head start on English before seventh grade, so she gave me lessons at no charge.

I also bugged my mom to buy me the tapes that the teacher used to teach us. They were recordings of Americans reading the English textbooks for each grade. It was unusual for me to nag my mom to buy me something since I knew our circumstances. But she bought them for me, and with the help of those tapes, I memorized most of the lessons in the seventh-grade English textbook before school started.

After I started seventh grade, the funniest thing happened in all of my middle school years. One of my classmates asked me if I had come from America, saying that there was a rumor like that going around. My English pronunciation reading the textbook was even better than the English teacher's—a Korean man—so he asked me to read the textbook in class every time. Since then, I was selected every year through high school to participate in Mokpo's English storytelling contest as the school's representative. I was also selected to compete at the county's English Eloquence contest a couple of times, and I won some prizes. But my mom was never able to come watch me, not even once.

I can recall a couple of other episodes related to English during my school years.

One time, I went to a convenience store and asked for instant coffee.

"Where is the coffee?"

The owner asked me, "What is it? I have never heard of it before."

"There's no way a grown-up doesn't know what coffee is. You know it, of course! Please show me where the coffee is!"

"I don't know what it is. I have never heard of it before. I wish I knew, but I don't know!"

I started to panic. "How come you don't know what coffee is? Coffee! Everybody knows, even children know!" The owner started to look desperate as well. I began explaining how to make the instant coffee by pouring it into hot water and that everybody drinks it daily.

Suddenly, I realized that I wasn't pronouncing it the Korean way. The Korean language doesn't have an "f" or "v." Immediately, I said it in the Korean way, and the owner exclaimed, "Oh, *keop'i*! That I know!"

Growing up in Korea, no matter how hard we studied English, we never spoke it outside of the classroom. We didn't even really speak it; we just learned to read and write. I wondered when I could ever use English.

So one day, when I was coming home from school, I noticed two white foreigners walking by a busy intersection in our small city. I stood there half-frozen, and my heart started to beat loudly in my ears. They stood out in the distance since they were so much taller than everyone else. I had always kept an eye out for foreigners, but to my frustration, I never saw one. It was a rare opportunity to meet foreigners and use my English.

I thought for a moment about giving up on it, but I couldn't let the chance pass by. So with all of the confidence I could muster, I approached them. I greeted them cheerfully in a loud voice, "How are you?" I didn't know what to say next, and I blushed in spite of my courage, but it made me feel so adventurous. I started to introduce myself.

The most unexpected thing happened as I was talking to foreigners. Before I knew it, we were surrounded by a crowd of people. The people who were passing by stopped and started to encircle us. All eyes were on me as if I were in a circus show with the two foreigners on the street. Had they never seen a young Korean girl talking to a foreigner in English before?

The foreigners realized it too. We stared at each other in surprise and slight fear. We were so shocked that we all broke out of the circle running together. We ran all the way back to their house and became friends until they left to visit some other regions for a couple of months.

Once I was in college, things became more difficult financially. To go to college in Korea, tuition had to be paid upfront in cash or by a personal check only. There were no loan systems like there are in America. Additionally, there were no grants or financial aid to help students from poorer backgrounds like myself. The only way to get extra money was through scholarships that could be earned after freshman year, but they weren't as easy for me as I had wished. Although I had A's for all classes related to my major, my other grades weren't good. On top of English, which was mandatory, we had to learn a third language. I switched back and forth between German and Spanish but did poorly in both. It was a blessing that I was able to go to college with my mom's savings, help from one of my aunts, and my part-time job, but it was impossible to continue my education without a scholarship.

When my husband proposed to me, I couldn't say anything but asked for some more time to think. After a couple of weeks, I decided to tell him the truth.

We met at a cafe near school but didn't talk much. Then I suggested that we take a walk, but I still couldn't say anything. Again, I suggested that we take a subway. I wanted to say it on the subway train, but I still couldn't. I wrestled with myself for almost two hours. It was the hardest thing I had ever done in any relationship, and I was losing confidence. I thought, *Why do I have to do this?* We arrived at Incheon, a harbor city near Seoul. He took me to the beach in a cab.

Strolling on the beach, I could breathe more easily and relax. It was already late in the afternoon. I finally spat out the word to him that I had been trying to say all day. It was my secret, my identity of shame: "*Saseng'a*" — a decent Korean word to describe a fatherless child. I told him that he was the first person in my life that I said the word to with my own mouth. I told him that if he was not bothered by it, I would marry him. I had seen enough soap operas to know that that word can tear apart relationships in Korea.

Surprisingly, it didn't bother him. But I had a second statement too: that the only condition under which I could marry him was that I needed to support my mom, so she needed to live with us. He agreed and said that after we went to America and settled there, we would bring her as soon as we could. I agreed as well. There was nothing Korea had to offer to keep me there.

I was only twenty-one years old when I came to America in 1989. My husband and I were young, poor immigrants and had to work very hard blue-collar jobs. While working so hard, I missed my mom terribly. Years were passing, and I worried every moment about her situation.

I had left her back in Korea, in my grandmother's house, to suffer alone at the hand of her real mother, who was my grandmother. I wished and prayed every day that my mom would be able to come and live with me. I was burdened with the responsibility of freeing her from Grandmother and supporting her. It was my ongoing mission from the start of my immigration.

Every time I went to church, there were visitors from Korea. Sometimes there was a long line to introduce the visiting families from Korea with endless welcoming applause. But my mom would not be able to come for another decade until 1999.

During the time I longed to be reunited with my mom, my two children were born, while my husband and I were also struggling to settle in a brand new country. And on top of that, I was being haunted by the memory of my witch-like grandmother. Every Sunday we went to church, the sermons were always about forgiveness, which frustrated me incredibly. It reminded me of my grandmother, but she was excluded from that category of forgiveness in my mind. I was tortured by the feeling that I had to forgive her.

In those days, my commute driving was my only personal time with God. In my first decade of living in America through my twenties, I started to consult with God about my problem. I told Him that I had no idea how to forgive my grandmother. If I had absolutely no desire to forgive her, how would I be able to do it?

I started to recognize my problem seriously and felt afraid of what God would think of me. I imagined God turning away from me and disowning me for my disobedience. It scared me more than anything else. Every time I prayed, I sobbed, devastated at the impossibility of forgiveness because I didn't have the desire, let alone the ability.

"Father! I want to do what You want me to do! But this, I can't. I wish I could do it, but I can't do what my heart can't do. I don't know how to forgive my grandmother. My heart can't. I can't help my heart. I can't! Forgive me, God! Help me, God! Make it happen in my heart so that I can do what You want me to do! Only if You make a miracle in my heart, then I will do it. Please make my heart do it. Please help me! I want to do what You want me to do! Please help!" I cried out sorrowfully to God like this every time. I cried out to Him constantly during my drive. I would be so engrossed in prayer that I would arrive at my destination before I even realized. My answer came twelve years later.

Two years after my mom's arrival in 1999, the most horrific thing occurred, a historic moment in America's history. The Twin Towers in New York City fell on September 11, 2001. Two days later, Wednesday morning of September 13, I received a phone call from Korea. One of my aunts called to tell me that my grandmother had passed away.

I was speechless from hearing the news. But even though I was surprised, I was not as surprised as I thought I should be, perhaps because it was just following the shock of 9/11. I stood there, waiting for more emotions to follow. I handed the phone to my mom, still anxious for more emotions about her passing to surprise me at any minute since I'm a very emotional person. Being too sensitive was always an issue for me, but not the opposite. I wasn't expecting to feel sadness since I was not affectionate towards my grandmother at all, so I was waiting for other familiar emotions to arise.

I waited for the feelings of discomfort, dizziness, and nausea to be followed by bitterness, fury, and wrath. These were the feelings I felt whenever I thought of my grandmother, as a rule. Her memory used to attack me, and pain would erupt like lava.

If I had a dream of her, then it was an awful nightmare of me trying to run away from a relentless evil, and I would wake up drenched in sweat. Any time I met someone who talked about their grandmother and childhood fondly, I would find a way to leave the conversation.

So when I heard of my grandmother's passing and felt nothing, I felt awkward. What happened to me that I felt nothing towards her? I tried to squeeze out any feelings I could about her passing.

But none of those bad feelings came. I was experiencing something I had never experienced before. A piece to the puzzle of my existence had vanished unexpectedly. I desperately searched to find the familiar contempt I harbored for my grandmother. Nothing surfaced. How could it be! This was uncharted territory. Realizing that my heart had been emptied of all of the negative emotions against my grandmother, a sparkling sensation spread in my head and heart. This was the work of God. Only He could sweep away and eliminate all evil out of my heart! There was no trace of it! I felt free. I felt so clean and so peaceful, with no pain from the memory of my grandmother. He made the impossible possible.

It was God's miracle in my heart; by His grace, I was set free. I was jumping with glee and screaming of joy! He answered my prayer of years to be able to forgive my grandmother and helped me do the one thing I could never do by myself. I am so free! Hallelujah, praise God!

Sometimes I get amazed, thinking about *why* I liked English and how I happened to come to America. These thoughts drove me to forgive my grandmother early in life. And the benefits of free communication in language drove me to attend an American, multicultural church. And I developed deep fellowship with American friends of all races in Christ. It's never easy to share deeply with Koreans because of cultural barriers and shame seeded in the culture, but it helped me to grow into who I am today. And behind all of these scenes, there has been a God who planned all of this for me.

I have swept away your offenses like a cloud, your sins like the morning mist. Return to me, for I have redeemed you.

Isaiah 44:22

So he said to me, "This is the word of the LORD to Zerubbabel: 'Not by might nor by power, but by my Spirit,' says the LORD Almighty."

Zechariah 4:6

For if you forgive other people when they sin against you, your heavenly Father will also forgive you.

Matthew 6:14

Then Peter came to Jesus and asked, "Lord, how many times shall I forgive my brother or sister who sins against me? Up to seven times?" Jesus answered, "I tell you, not seven times, but seventy-seven times."

Matthew 18:21–22

This is my blood of the covenant, which is poured out for many for the forgiveness of sins.

Matthew 26:28

Jesus said, "Father, forgive them, for they do not know what they are doing." And they divided up his clothes by casting lots.

Luke 23:34

5. Non-Stop Love

Time flew by like an arrow, and before I knew it, it was 2017. As the years passed, I stopped thinking about my grandmother and became caught up in my life and children growing up. They were all grown up in an instant, within the blink of an eye, right in front of my eyes. My son was twenty-six and dependable, and my baby daughter—she will always be—was twenty-one, a senior in college.

My husband always seemed to try to hold them from growing up, only adoring them more, and I felt confident that my children and I were very close, without any big secrets in our lives. Our children are our pride.

But something happened with my daughter that I felt like I was stabbed in the back. I believed my baby, my daughter, too much. She was a high honor roll student and a coach and mentor on her debate team. Whoever knows her knows she is a smart one.

I remembered that behind all scenes, there is spiritual warfare—an enemy—and if we don't recognize it, it's almost impossible to win over it.

The Bible describes our opponents as spiritual enemies who want to steal, kill, and destroy us and our relationship with God (John 10:10) and make us lose sight of His purpose for us.

Be alert and of sober mind. Your enemy the dev-

il prowls around like a roaring lion looking for someone to devour.

1 Peter 5:8

For our struggle is not against flesh and blood, but against the rulers, against the authorities, against the powers of this dark world and against the spiritual forces of evil in the heavenly realms.

Ephesians 6:12

The evening meal was in progress, and the devil had already prompted Judas, the son of Simon Iscariot, to betray Jesus.

John 13:2

One very late night towards the end of March 2017, she confessed to me about her secret boyfriend after I pressed her a bit. She said it was her choice, and she did not regret it. I felt my heart shattering into pieces at the revelation.

I know what people would say in this day and age: "What's wrong?", "What's the big deal?" I know everyone is different with their own stories, and I have plenty of my own as well. But my children and I had all been baptized and were committed to the Lord, and since they were young, we prayed together at least a few times a week. We had prayed for so many things together. They had seen their mom's tears and wiped up those tears. They were my God-given praying partners at home. I had raised them to be different and distinguished from the world, to have a relationship with God, not like I had been at their age. While my husband had resisted a relationship with God and being a spiritual team, my children had always been so obedient to my solo leadership at home. I had been so grateful and so proud of them.

But that night, the enemy threw a bomb at me, and I was burnt on the spot. With all my strength, I came back to life and asked her my first question about her boyfriend, "Is he a Christian?" He wasn't. I felt betrayed. My daughter did not say sorry to God or me, only defending her faith.

"Only a Christian believer" was my one and only condition as a mother for her future boyfriend and spouse. But on top of that, he wasn't even a U.S. citizen. Nothing about him was in any of the categories I ever even imagined for my daughter.

I heard the enemy laughing at me loudly, and I fell apart helplessly.

Oh, God, help me! Father, why did You allow the enemy to do this to my daughter? Where were You? Didn't I pray about her boyfriend? How much did I pray? Oh, Father, help me to not fail this test. Oh, my Father, please help me handle this right!

It was the cruelest and most devastating night to me since she was born.

I sobbed until 5 a.m. when I finally laid my head on my pillow. For the first time, I wished I had had no children, but I repented to God immediately for that thought and thanked Him endlessly for keeping her safe and well, for God had reminded me of a story that I heard of a local Korean pastor whose college daughter had been murdered a couple of years ago. *Oh God, I'm sorry, I'm so sorry! Forgive me, forgive me! Thank You, thank You for sparing my daughter's life!*

My husband was asleep as usual. I couldn't tell him for a few days. Since then, my family was attacked and brokenhearted. King Solomon's wisdom rang loudly in my ears, "'Meaningless! Meaningless!' says the teacher. 'Utterly meaningless! Everything is meaningless'" (Ecclesiastes 1:1).

In church the following Sunday, I sat alone in my seat. I didn't sit at my usual place in the front of the sanctuary but in the furthest back row. I wept quietly through our praise and worship service. I sensed an old lady from far away approaching me, and she hugged the person right in front of me. The old lady and I had never greeted each other before since we usually sat far away, even though we were both at church every Sunday. As she turned away from the person in front of me, surprisingly, she hugged me next. It was abrupt, but with a soft smile, she extended a greeting and then walked away slowly. This kind of greeting is common in my church—we are a multicultural church with an extremely open culture, with lots of hugging, greeting anyone and everyone in the Lord.

The Holy Spirit spoke to me to follow her. Immediately, I asked her if I could talk to her, so we moved to the ladies' room, where we were alone. She was almost a stranger to me, but I knew that I could tell her everything. I begged her while sobbing to pray for my daughter. Instead of praying right away, amazingly, she began to gently chastise and exhort me. The Holy Spirit spoke to me through her: that all I have to do is love my daughter unconditionally, more than ever before, never correcting her or arguing with her, but only showing her my love. *Wow, I needed this, Lord, thank You!* She added that I just needed to pray to God and trust Him. God provided me the perfect guidance through my fellow church lady, who I had never talked to before. For this whole time, nobody stopped by the ladies' room.

On Tuesday, my small group meeting approached. I could sense the enemy's trap against me more strongly. I found myself wanting to quit my small group because I didn't want to share with them what was going on with my daughter. I felt like I was dragged to the small group that day, and even while I sang the opening praise song with the group, I was still wrestling inside. *God, please let this pass from me. I can't share this with my group. I can't. I can't. I'm so humiliated. Let me just pretend like nothing happened. Please let this pass from me. I don't want to share about my daughter with my group, please!* But before I knew it, I was already confessing my problem to the group. Thank God. God knew that

I couldn't go through this season without prayer. My group was truly God's provided support.

So I chose to trust God ever so closely, at every minute, to not fall apart in a season of aggressive transition. There were no other options for me. I drudged through that season senselessly with my broken heart. Time seemed to stop, not ticking forward, no matter what I did. Vaguely, I felt I was getting better. God was working, though I couldn't see or perceive it. Since the spring, I was holding on to Him as if we were hovering over the ocean after a storm, not knowing when I would touch the ground.

Life seemed so meaningless. I couldn't help but feel useless, and the enemy kept telling me that I have no purpose in my life, which is no different from a non-believer's experience. Although I believed in His promises, the enemy was so strong. My tears rolled down my face frequently, but God never left me alone. Tenderly, He was putting back together all of the pieces of my shattered heart, one by one.

Surprisingly, I found comfort through divine appointments with my massage clients constantly. In the past, God had sent me clients who I comforted and ministered to. But in this season, things were awkwardly reversed. My working appointments became my healing sessions. I had no clue and never planned such sessions, but somehow the Holy Spirit always intervened for me to be prayed for by my stranger clients by touching their hearts and opening them up to pray, even through our short conversations; there was a female pastor, another born-again Christian, and some angelic sisters in God. The Lord comforted me in such tangible ways that the world could never imagine.

Even though God sent me comfort, I wavered back and forth, not able to heal completely. I searched for ways to stabilize my heart, looking for any kind of answer to help me, but no matter how hard I prayed, I did not receive any guidance on how to move forward. There was nothing I could do, nothing, but to trust God. This was the conclusion that I reached at the time, that I had to give everything up to God: "Come to me, all you who are weary and burdened, and I will give you rest" (Matthew 11:28), and "Submit yourselves, then, to God. Resist the devil, and he will flee from you" (James 4:7).

I surrendered my daughter to God. I let her go to the One who is most concerned about her. My burden seemed to lift away from me. This time, I didn't want to take the burden back, not like all of the other times I raised her up temporarily. *She's not mine, but Yours! I trust You!* I kept giving her to Him, to give her fully to the Lord, knowing that God would never leave nor forsake her (Hebrews 13:5), and believing that God would work out all things for her good (Romans 8:28). I was reminded that He even has an unbelievably wonderful plan for her life (Jeremiah 29:11).

Even though I gave her up to God, I could still love

her with all I have! I could finally breathe comfortably, without any more pain in my chest, and I felt as light as a feather. Wherever I went, I encountered His presence. The bright and warm colors of the trees' flowers and leaves soothed my soul. My heart was filled with His peace. It was such an unforgettable comparison to my past when I prayed for my depression, which was finally answered. I could remember years of not really sensing or experiencing the seasons and the pure beauty of God's creation due to the enormous stress of an immigrants' life. Furthermore, the worst times in my early life had passed decades ago. There was so much to be thankful for, and God humbled me with His faithfulness.

Soon after that, one Friday, I was doing a massage at the spa that I worked at in late October 2017. Calming and soothing my client and myself, I also exhaled as I directed her to breathe out. It was a smooth and quiet session until I noticed something unusual. When the client turned over to lie on her back, I almost jumped away from the table. I quickly rearranged the bolster and sheets as she turned, but I kept blinking my eyes and shaking my head to calm myself. Maybe it was a problem with the light? It was too dim in the room, so it could have been a hallucination. How could I have seen my grandmother in my client's face?

I hadn't thought of her for so long. I hadn't been thinking of anything related to her, just praying and meditating on God during my massage as usual. I was reciting Bible verses: "The Lord is my shepherd, I lack nothing. He makes me lie down in green pastures, he leads me beside quiet waters, he refreshes my soul" (Psalm 23:1–3). "Do not be anxious about anything, but in every situation, by prayer and petition, with thanksgiving, present your requests to God. And the peace of God, which transcends all understanding, will guard your hearts and minds in Christ Jesus" (Philippians 4:6–7). "Whoever dwells in the shelter of the Most High will rest in the shadow of the Almighty" (Psalm 91:1).

So it was absolute nonsense to me that I saw my Asian grandmother's face in my Caucasian client's. Suddenly at the thought of her, my heart began to pound, and my back began to sweat. I shook my head again, asking God to help me. I wanted to just snap out of it. My hands and body worked on their own, and I closed my eyes. I felt like my mind flew out of my body at the speed of light into a sea of memories a million miles away.

How old was she then? My grandmother! She passed away in 2001, two days after 9/11. The earliest memory I had of her was when I was five years old going to kindergarten, just when my grandfather had passed away. She was quite young to be a widow herself, still having three unmarried children with her asides from me and my mom. I started mentally calculating her age: she could have been about fifty since my mom gave birth to me at the age of twenty-eight, and I was five, which made my mom around thirty-three. Grandmother probably bore my mom, the oldest, at seventeen or eighteen, as her generation used to start at that young age. Then she was about my age now when she had become a widow. I felt a chill. For the first time in my life, I felt connected to her.

Was she lost at the loss of her husband? Was she lonely? Was she miserable? Was she completely devastated with so many burdens?

I closed my eyes even harder to observe her better. She was sitting, holding her head in her hands in the edge of darkness, in my mental screen. Closing my eyes more tightly, I was seeing her ever so closely through the eyes of my heart. My heart filled up quickly, perceiving her pain, which I had never imagined before.

Had she become an alcoholic immediately then, or since before? I had no clue. *Had she been depressed then? Why hadn't I known that? I could have comforted her! But I didn't know anything. I was only a child. I didn't know that, Lord! How could I know? Nobody told me, not even my mom. I was only a child! If I had known her pain and sorrow, I could have been better for her. I could have loved her!*

My tears were streaming down my cheeks. I desperately wanted to touch her as I was watching her mentally. My body wanted to jump into the scene to hug her tightly. Internally, I wailed at her pain, shoulders shaking, and I almost fell over my client.

Wake up! I shook my head again, taking an extra-large gulp of breath, and wiped my tears stealthily. Mentally a mess, I barely managed to finish the session.

I could not tell my mom what happened to me for more than a week. I was overwhelmed and not only had to process what had happened but also understand why and how it happened. When I was alone in my room, unbelievably, I was still wailing and weeping at my grandmother's pain, which I had never even thought about before. The brand new compassion towards my grandmother in me was a fresh shock to acknowledge because I know that I didn't have the capacity in me before.

Just being able to forgive my grandmother for my mom's life and mine had been a miracle for me back in 2001. It happened only by the grace of God, as a miracle in which God cleaned out my negative emotions against her and made my heart clean.

After that, every once in a while, whenever I thought of her, I wondered over and over again: did God love her? I know it can sound so childish, but my perception of her was so limited and confined like a prison cell, so I could only laugh at myself.

But now, God opened the door of that cell and widened my perception of her, freeing the eyes of my heart to see her through His eyes. It was like a great discovery to me. *Ah! Now I know! Oh God, You loved her so much! Wow!*

Gratefully overwhelmed, I was singing the last praise song during Sunday worship. When I saw the following lyrics on the projector screen at the altar, as I followed the song, my heart was bursting: "I want to know your heart, I want to know your heart! I surrender!"

I could not believe what God had done for me. He allowed me to peek into His heart, to know His heart! I saw His heart, and it is so full of love. He loved my grandmother, who I could never even imagine loving, and had just barely forgiven. I almost wanted to shout out to everybody: "I know His heart! God made me know His heart! I looked into His heart!" I sobbed at His amazing gift for me.

What a revelation from God! Furthermore, God was expanding my discernment for His love towards my daughter. I have known His love for us, which is unfailing and unchanging (Isaiah 54:10; Hebrews 6:17), praying that very verse numerous times. But I had been sorry to God about my daughter for what she had done. I couldn't stop feeling somewhat guilty since the spring, and I asked that I would be punished in her stead.

Instead, I was refreshed by the revelation of the Holy Spirit, and I perceived in my heart what this was all about. His vast love for my daughter was just immeasurable. He reassured me that His love is not like mine, shattered so easily. His love is beyond my imagination and has never changed towards her. He never stopped loving me or her. Wow!

The revelation of His massive love put my broken heart back together instantly and completely, like a miracle glue. My season of painful transition was over. It was the perfect, unbelievably intimate gift from God's heart to mine. The grace of God showered me to make me more than a conqueror (Romans 8:37). He made me so free from all the shame and guilt I felt.

"Though the mountains be shaken and the hills be removed, yet my unfailing love for you will not be shaken nor my covenant of peace be removed" *says the LORD, who has compassion on you.*

Isaiah 54:10

The thief comes only to steal and kill and destroy; I have come that they may have life, and have it to the full.

John 10:10

Every good and perfect gift is from above, coming down from the Father of the heavenly lights, who does not change like shifting shadows.

James 1:17

No, in all these things we are more than conquerors through him who loved us.

Romans 8:37

And we know that in all things God works for the good of those who love him, who have been called according to his purpose.

Romans 8:28

For I am convinced that neither death nor life, neither angels nor demons, neither the present nor the future, nor any powers, neither height nor depth, nor anything else in all creation, will be able to separate us from the love of God that is in Christ Jesus our Lord.

Romans 8:38

Because God wanted to make the unchanging nature of his purpose very clear to the heirs of what was promised, he confirmed it with an oath.

Hebrews 6:17

My Father

They will rebuild the ancient ruins and restore the places long devastated; they will renew the ruined cities that have been devastated for generations.

Isaiah 61:4

For I, the LORD, love justice; I hate robbery and wrongdoing. In my faithfulness I will reward my people and make an everlasting covenant with them.

Isaiah 61:8

1. My Mom's Lie

The night after I heard my grandmother criticize me, I was afraid to ask my mom about my father. I was afraid, but I needed to hear the truth from my mom. She will never be able to imagine how much courage it took for me to ask her about him at the young age that I did. I asked her slowly and carefully why I didn't have a father. It was the first time I ever asked her such a question. I remember her answer clearly: "Although you don't have your earthly father to touch and talk with, you have God, and that God in heaven wants to be a true Father to you and to everyone. So you can call Him 'Father,' 'Dad,' 'Father God in heaven,' freely, anytime you want. He is Almighty, so He can see and hear you all the time, even though you can't see or hear Him. So call on Him and talk to God whenever you miss your dad and want to talk to him. You can just talk to Him in your head and from your heart even without speaking. He can hear you all the time!"

Wow! My chin dropped in awe as I listened to her, that I could call God my father. It blew me away, and I was filled with glee. My mom had no idea how cool she had sounded. It was the perfect answer for a five-year-old, and it was so fascinating, so I didn't need any other explanations. Somehow, it satisfied my young soul.

I immediately started to talk to God, unceasingly asking Him the thousands of questions that I had carried daily that I couldn't ask my mom or anybody. I told Him how I missed my earthly father and asked Him all the things I couldn't understand about my grandmother's household.

I had no other choice, really, since I had no one else I could talk to. Though my mom stayed in the house, she was busy tailoring all day long and never told me any fun stories or took me anywhere. I had almost no extracurricular programs outside of school, so I was all alone, with no siblings or steady playmates, living in inexplicable solitude. Every day was so long and so boring.

Other than God, I talked to the trees, flowers, and other plants. We had a sizable garden with vegetables and trees that grew figs, grapes, and cherries, and flowers for every season, including forsythias, daffodils, azaleas, roses, sage, cosmoses, and hydrangeas. The city of Mokpo, where we lived, is at the southwest end of the peninsula, so the climate is warm enough to grow fig trees. We had two large fig trees in the garden. I ate the largest, fattest, sweetest figs all the time. My favorite fruit is Korean concord grapes, but I miss the figs I ate in my childhood.

In the middle of the garden, there was a small pond with goldfish. Once when I was in kindergarten, I fell into that pond. Though I wasn't hurt, I got soaked and was spooked by the large goldfish that swam up to me. I avoided going near the pond after I fell.

Since my grandfather was a beekeeper, he grew flowers for the bees. After he passed away, Grandmother continued his work. I was stung by bees three or four times growing up—on my lips, the bottom of my foot (I stepped on a bee barefoot in the summertime), and my arm.

As time passed like this, I got into the habit of talking to Father God naturally every day, just as there were clouds in the sky and wind in the air. But I also started to miss my father even more severely. It was worse every time I played with the other kids in my town.

Children would play outside of their homes from dawn to dusk in the summer. We didn't have a playground, so we just played outside. I wasn't an athletic child, but I desperately wanted to be included, especially when I was in the lower grades. I sought opportunities to play with them and was grateful to be included. We played all day with no sense of time.

At the end of the day, their mothers would start calling them in for dinner. The children didn't care and kept playing.

But one mother called out again, "Your father is here." Surprisingly, that child stopped playing immediately and ran home joyfully. Another mom called out the same, "Your dad is here!" The number of children decreased gradually until, before I knew it, everyone was gone at their father's arrival, and I was left alone.

This happened time after time. I wished I could hear my mom calling, "Your dad is here."

A year or two passed since I had asked my mom about my father. But I was itching to ask about him once more, feeling as if the question could bring him home to see me. My mom must have sensed my depression because she told me that he would come home once I entered middle school. He would come from America, where he was making money. I was exhilarated by the news and boasted to the other kids that my father would come from America with lots and lots of gifts for me once I started middle school. It became my dream. Entering middle school seemed so far away.

Then, I began second grade. My mom had to talk to a Father at the Catholic church for a meeting, so I waited outside the door. I was able to hear some of what she was telling the Father. I couldn't believe my ears, because I heard a big bad word: divorce. My mom told the Father that she was divorced.

As a second-grader in the '70s, "divorce" was a bad word. I trembled with shame and felt sorry for my mom. I began putting thoughts together like a detective, searching for clues to get the answer I needed. My mom was divorced, which meant she was separated from my father permanently, or my father deserted us.

Then what my mom had told me was a lie. Everything was a lie. He would not come back to me even if I entered middle school, and he hadn't wanted to see me once all that time. He didn't want my mom or me. Why would I want a father like that? I thought, "I don't need him anymore." I decided not to miss him anymore. It was my turn to erase him from my life. He had never existed in my life anyways. The father who didn't want me was not needed by me either. My father was dead to me.

2. My School Experiences

I don't have many enjoyable memories of school. It was just another environment that I had to survive. Everything in school was about competition. From middle school to high school, there was a bulletin board that announced the rank of every student after every test. Even in elementary school, report cards displayed grades and rank. Rankings determined your worth compared to everyone else. There wasn't any emphasis on teamwork; academics was a lonely race.

When I did well on a test, I was proud, but when I didn't, I was humiliated. I was treated as a number or a rank more than anything else. Every grown-up around me asked, "What is your ranking at school?" It seemed like that was everyone's only concern.

When my children began school in America, I never saw their rank on their report cards or school bulletin, which made me wonder about it every once in a while. I asked their teachers, but they just wondered why I wanted to know my child's ranking in the school when their academic progress was very satisfactory.

But, while I hated rankings growing up, there was something else I hated even more. And no matter how much I hated it, I could never avoid it because there was no advance notice. It was the official annual household survey.

At the time, the country was recovering from the

Korean War (1950–1953) and developing rapidly through the '70s and '80s, when I was attending school. Maybe household statistics were the most straightforward way for the government to figure out the status of the nation's wellbeing. And children are innocent and honest, so they must have been an easy and accurate group to survey.

They surveyed us verbally, not on paper. Did they not have paper to use? I could only assume that they didn't care about protecting children's privacy or emotions. So the hour-long survey of at least fifty questions was conducted the same way, over and over again, for twelve years: the assigned teacher would enter the classroom, stand behind the pulpit, and, without any consideration, begin asking the same questions every year.

The majority of teachers performed the task mindlessly, showing neither proof of training for the survey nor any sign of understanding of primary-school-age psychology as educators. They must have thought they were offering a fun time for the children as they made each inquiry loudly from the pulpit, "Raise your hand if you have a car at home," "Raise your hand if you have a piano at home," "Raise your hand if you have a TV at home." Children "oo-ed" and "ah-ed" at the wealth of students who raised their hands high for those questions. For a piano, maybe five or more students raised their hands. But in a class of sixty to seventy, only one or two hands ever went up for a car, and many times no one raised their hand since my hometown was only a small city.

Those who could raise their hands for such luxury items did so proudly, with a wide grin on their faces, as if they had been waiting for this unique opportunity to boast. But those who could only watch others raise their hands continuously looked envious at the sudden revelation of their own poverty. Wealth was measured materialistically, using every piece of electronics available then, from a car to a toaster.

Without any warning, the teacher suddenly moved on to the next portion of the survey. Without any change in tone or expression, they said, "Raise your hand if you don't have a father."

The students seemed to go quiet. Who would want to raise their hand for such a question in public? I felt like I was having a mini heart attack at the prospect of having to raise my hand. I fought with myself for the lie I could choose to tell.

God, must I do this? Don't I have a choice not to do this? I wanted to run away, but my body felt frozen. I was never the first one to raise my hand for that question. To my amazement, one person's hand would go up, and then another. I was in awe of their courage.

It was so cruel. I was still fighting internally, but I was compelled to support them. Spurred by the other volunteers, I gave myself up hopelessly. With all of my strength, I decided to detach my arm from my body, just for this moment.

My classmates all searched around them for the hands that went up, turning their heads 360 degrees as if they were a radar to help the teacher out. Sensing all eyes on me, I raised my hand slowly and blushed breathlessly. It was the cruelest thing the school did to children like me every year. I hated those insensitive teachers.

I could also hear the hushed whispers of the other students' gossiping. They expressed their surprise about me as the survey continued.

The second question was easier. "Raise your hand if you don't have a mother." Now, I was able to breathe, and I peeked around the room for those hands, very carefully and respectfully, pretending not to look. I wanted to know who they were for a different reason than that of the other children who gossiped about me: if I was allowed, I wanted to comfort them. I still remember when I met the eyes of those who didn't have a father or mother, exchanging a look of mutual empathy and sympathy, as if silently saying, "You are not alone."

After the survey, a few friends came over to comfort me, saying, "I'm so sorry about your father, I didn't know." I felt another rush of embarrassment, but I overcame it by pretending to be indifferent. On the other hand, there was always a group of mean children who would boast about their parents' wealth right in front of me. They regarded me with condescension and disdain. I had no value to them.

Even worse than the children, though, was the eventual realization that this heartless procedure was a tool for educators to measure and judge everyone according to what they had.

But once in a while, there were good, truly good teachers who understood compassion and consideration. They had the wisdom to say, "Everybody, put your head down on your desk. Close your eyes. Nobody is looking; just raise your hand!" Thank God! Those teachers made such a difference. I admired and thanked them in my mind. They were my heroes.

When I was in the second grade, the entire school was practicing for our annual fall festival for parents and visitors to come watch each grade perform a coordinated dance. For weeks, the entire playground was filled with children from every grade practicing. Teachers led groups of hundreds of students in the motions for their grade's dance. The noise was overwhelming.

I was a tall child, so I was placed at the very back of the line, far from the front where our teacher stood. She was too far away for me to understand her instructions. Before I knew it, I became immersed in the fifth-grade class' dance, which was taking place right next to me. They were using props like hand-held fans, which fascinated me.

Suddenly, *wham!* I felt like I had been struck by lightning and fell to the ground. My cheek burned, and my head spun as I saw stars around me. I didn't know what happened, and I couldn't get up. Then, I realized Mrs. Choi was towering over me, her eyes flashing with anger as she hollered at me.

Mrs. Choi was my class teacher, who was leading my grade in our dance at the very front. Unbelievably, she had run up to me at full speed and hit my face for not paying attention to her.

She continued to stand over me, yelling at me with a horrific expression, but I couldn't hear her as I wailed loudly. It was unbearably painful as my head pounded into my ears, but I was even more shocked with shame and humiliation.

Although my grandmother beat my mom at home with her bare hands right in front of me a countless number of times, she had never beaten me once. So being beaten by my teacher at school was so shameful to me. It wasn't uncommon for teachers to physically discipline their students, but this was my first time being hit by someone's bare hand, and despite it not being uncommon, it was the first and the last time for me.

After the incident, I realized what hurt me the most was that Mrs. Choi knew me and my mom better than any other teacher in the entire school. Even though my mom didn't ever come to school and wasn't a member of the parents' committee, Mrs. Choi and her family attended the same Catholic church we attended. Her son was in the same grade as me at school, and we attended Saturday children's school together. She knew who I was as a fatherless child.

I was so ashamed of this event, I couldn't tell my mom what had happened, but I could never forget it either. I had trusted my teachers and even dreamed of becoming one, but I was completely betrayed in that moment. Even before this incident, I was a very good student, often being the class leader and earning some achievements and certificates, but from then on, I worked even harder to prove myself to her.

Although some teachers like Mrs. Choi changed their attitudes after reading my birth certificate, some encouraged me even more warmly. Ironically, Mrs. Choi's husband was my middle school teacher, and he was always consistently kind to me.

Then the next year, my third-grade teacher was Mr. Oh. For some reason, this teacher adored me. During storytime, we sat around in a circle on the floor. He often put one student on his lap on his chair as a special treat. At this time, this kind of physical attention was normal and not any reason for concern. But when he called me and put me on his lap, I couldn't enjoy it at all, and he called me quite often. Sometimes I hid from him, but surprisingly, he always found me.

Though he was gentle and kind throughout the year, I couldn't process his kindness. Perhaps it was because of all the trauma that I experienced continuously at home. I just wondered why he was so caring to me, and all of his attention made me feel uncomfortable.

Years later, after I became a mom and a teacher at Sunday school, I realized that Mr. Oh had treated me like his own daughter. I couldn't get used to it back then because, in addition to being a very shy girl, I had never had that kind of affection from any male figure in my life except my grandfather, but my memory of him was vague, and he passed away so long ago.

In fact, his actual daughter was in the same grade as me in a different class. Whenever she stopped by for an errand to my class, Mr. Oh didn't let her go without having her sing a song for us. She earned prizes in many singing contests, so she always sang beautifully for us as her dad played the organ. I felt sorry for her, that her dad gave me special treatment, while also envying her for having such a good father. Later we became friends. I wish I could meet him now and thank him for his special love and care for me.

Despite the trauma that some teachers left on me in the past, God's power and grace have enabled me to forgive them. So the recollections above are only memories and facts from the past. I know there are complicated and severe matters that we can't forgive with ease because our flesh hates to do so. Rather, we want revenge, as our human nature and weaknesses. However, I have experienced that God enables me to do things that I can't—such as the forgiveness of my grandmother—as long as I want to, no matter how long it takes.

Forgiveness is a choice and privilege for those who have experienced and accepted the love of God, who gave us His Son Jesus, who is sinless and spotless, as a sacrifice for us sinners. Jesus is risen and alive. I am forgiven eternally because God forgave me, the sinner, through Jesus (Hebrews 10:14). I live because He lives!

When they hurled their insults at him, he did not retaliate; when he suffered, he made no threats. Instead, he entrusted himself to him who judges justly.

1 Peter 2:23

But he was pierced for our transgressions, he was crushed for our iniquities; the punishment that brought us peace was on him, and by his wounds we are healed.

Isaiah 53:5

For if you forgive other people when they sin against you, your heavenly Father will also forgive you. But if you do not forgive others their sins, your Father will not forgive your sins.

Matthew 6:14–15

3. A Culture of Shame

There was a girl named Abigail in my son's second-grade class in about 1999. She was a handicapped child in a wheelchair and was able to write with her weakly developed hand and arm.

I visited his class for a couple of hours weekly as a helping mom. Although I wanted to help her, I realized that she had a personal assistant who did everything for her, from helping with schoolwork to driving her to and from home. It was an astonishing thing for me to witness, as an immigrant, the level of special care in this country.

When we came home together on those days, I asked my son, "Do you help Abigail sometimes when she needs help?" He answered, "Sure I do, Mom! We all help her. Why do you ask?" I had to laugh, and I rubbed his head, telling him I was so proud of him. He murmured that my question was silly. He didn't know what his mom was thinking. I was relieved by his loving heart and mature attitude, but I still felt an ache in my heart for my friends back in my elementary school in the late '70s.

A couple of years later, it was my son's middle school graduation. The graduation was held in a huge arena out of town due to our high school renovation. Children entered in a long line towards the stage. Parents sitting on chairs and on the staircases surrounding the arena applauded with shouts and whistles as the children entered.

Suddenly, the cheering turned into a standing ovation for one person, a tiny girl. It was Abigail, at the end of a long line of children, who had decided to walk on that day. Although she was very slow, she was able to walk. I sobbed and applauded, thanking God!

"Fatherless" was a taboo word in the Korean society I grew up in. As soon as people discovered my "label," they frowned and turned their noses up at me and would gossip with each other right in front of me in lowered voices. Many of my teachers looked at me with embarrassment and changed their attitudes upon seeing my birth record, which shows a blank in the column for my father's name and also my mom's record of divorce. It was like my fatherlessness offended them. I experienced this kind of judgment and disgust across all of the people I knew, including my closest relatives, neighbors, and teachers. Knowledge of my identity gave people some kind of unspoken authority over me. And there was no concept or theory that I could rely on then to resist their unfair and cruel treatment. Shame was just shame.

"Fatherless" was not the only shameful label then. Other taboo groups included orphans, handicaps, sin-

gle mothers, and more. Growing up in Korea, I witnessed all of these groups suffer discrimination and
abuse. Orphans were despised, the handicapped were
shunned, and single mothers were slandered. They
were cast out as shameful, abnormal, and detrimental
to society.

These examples above are why I call Korean culture "a culture of shame." The root of this shame and
discrimination is related to Korean Confucianism and
the classism that existed for five hundred years in the
Korean dynasty until the beginning of the twentieth
century. There were four classes then: the dynasty,
nobles, commoners, and slaves. Relationships were
measured vertically within and by these four classes.
Within each class, people could improve their rank or
position to become more important than others in their
class. For example, nobles strove to attain high-plac-
ing jobs within the government to upgrade their social
ranking. After passing the exam and earning their position, they would live and die with that title. However,
outside of marriage between the dynasty and nobles,
there was no upward mobility between classes. People could be punished and thrown into a lower class,
but the system was strict with slaves and commoners.
They could never dream of rising above their class.

This way of viewing relations vertically allowed
people to look down on commoners, slaves, and any
people that didn't seem "normal" or offered uncer-
tainty to others that they came from a respectable

background. People would go as far as to abuse and discriminate against these groups as a way to protect societal order.

I believe that even after classism ended, people were so used to the societal stability that the vertical ranking of relationships seemed to bring that they found new ways to order themselves vertically. Nowadays, when most Korean people meet a new person, they conduct an informal "survey" where they ask the person about their age and job. Outwardly, the questions we hear are "How old are you?" and "What do you do for a living?" but inwardly, I think the real question they are trying to answer is "Are you above or below me?" So instead of the four classes, they use age, sex, and occupation to establish a vertical relationship.

The influence of Confucianism, classism, and vertical relationships are visible in modern Korean society since, culturally, people in Korea don't call each other by their first names unless they are family or very close friends. They only call other people by their job titles, "Teacher," "Doctor," "Judge," etc.

Years ago, the principal of my children's elementary school was my nail client. At the school, she was called Dr. Smith, so that was what I called her when she came to my nail salon. She corrected me and asked me to call her by her first name, Mary. It wasn't easy to call her by her first name since my children were attending her school. After she begged me multiple times on different occasions, I finally gave in and called her Mary. I experienced this many times in America, people asking me to call them by their name when they were outside of their office, whether they were doctors, police officers, or attorneys. It was important to them that I acknowledged who they were, not what they were.

This mindset is contrary to the culture created by Confucianism, which is only concerned with familial and societal order, not equality. Nobody cares about who you are, but only what you are from birth or the titles you earn.

How is everything above related to the story of my nonexistent father?

It was the main reason my life was affected by my fatherlessness, creating an unavoidable stigma of shame. Again, I realized all of this only after coming to America and seeing the difference in how people reacted to ideas I thought were normally shameful.

In the '90s, when I was working in a Korean nail salon in my twenties, there was a young client around my age who told me she was a fatherless child, not knowing her biological father. She told me this freely and unashamedly, which shocked me.

That was only the beginning. I saw all kinds of American people speaking about everything unashamedly. And what amazed me even more was the attitude of people who listened. They reacted with love and kindness. This happened again and again, and not only within churches.

They didn't know that fatherlessness, the handicapped, orphans, single mothers, and so many others were an embarrassment in the culture I grew up in, where those things were taught to be viewed as shameful. None of my American friends could even understand my history of shame. The culture they grew up in didn't seem to teach those things as being shameful, so they didn't discriminate against their unfortunate background.

There is a story in the Bible about a woman who was caught in adultery (John 8:3–11). Jews were about to kill a woman with stones according to the law. But Jesus stepped in and told them that the person without any sin should throw the first stone. The people left, one by one.

It is written that God created both men and women according to His image (Genesis 1:27). So everyone is valuable to Him. No one can judge another person's value before God.

And God told us to love each other throughout the Scriptures. Furthermore, He even specified His special love for the fatherless, orphans, widows, the blind, the deaf, the crippled, the lepers, and all those who were weak and outcasts of society.

God has been with me at all times. Nevertheless, there have been times when I was blinded and could not see or admit His love because I had been so hurt, stubborn, and dumb. But His love chased after me unfailingly until I gave in to it.

How could I be set free from all of the shame within me, holding me hostage for decades? It should have been impossible; there is absolutely no medicine or remedy in the world to cure shame.

But I have felt God's fervent love for me personally because God emphasized that He becomes a Father to the fatherless so many times throughout the Bible. Psalm 10:17–18: "You listen to their cry, defending the fatherless and the oppressed"; Psalm 68:5: "A father to the fatherless, a defender of widows, is God in his holy dwelling"; Psalm 82:3: "Defend the weak and the fatherless; uphold the cause of the poor and the oppressed"; Psalm 27:10: "Though my father and mother forsake me, the Lord will receive me"; Deuteronomy 10:18: "He defends the cause of the fatherless and the widow, and loves the foreigner residing among you"; Zechariah 7:10: "Do not oppress the widow or the fatherless, the foreigner or the poor. Do not plot evil against each other"; Malachi 3:5:

"So I will come to put you on trial. I will be quick to testify against sorcerers, adulterers and perjurers, against those who defraud laborers of their wages, who oppress the widows and the fatherless, and deprive the foreigners among you of justice, but do not fear me," says the Lord Almighty.

God's tender love chased me unceasingly, never giving up on me. How could I not be touched and cured by His tremendous love?

I wouldn't be able to break free from the emotional and spiritual chains that hold me down on my own. But I was bathed in His outpouring love and healed. Hallelujah!

So I thank God, and I praise Him with all of myself for all of my life to eternity.

> *As for those who were held in high esteem—whatever they were makes no difference to me; God does not show favoritism—they added nothing to my message.*
> **Galatians 2:6**

> *So in Christ Jesus you are all children of God through faith, for all of you who were baptized into Christ have clothed yourselves with Christ.*
> **Galatians 3:26–27**

> *The Spirit you received does not make you slaves, so that you live in fear again; rather, the Spirit you received brought about your adoption to sonship. And by him we cry, "Abba, Father." The Spirit himself testifies with our spirit that we are God's children.*
> **Romans 8:15–16**

Then Peter began to speak: "I now realize how true it is that God does not show favoritism."

Acts 10:34

Do not judge, and you will not be judged. Do not condemn, and you will not be condemned. Forgive, and you will be forgiven.

Luke 6:37

I want to share a lighthearted episode that contrasts American and Korean culture.

Many years ago, I watched a talent show at my children's elementary school for the first time. In Korean, a talent show is called *Hakyehoe*. However, *Hakyehoe* is a very special show in Korea. The performers are proven gifted and talented children who have already won prizes and awards outside of school. So when I attended my children's elementary school's talent show, I was shocked at first and didn't understand the level of quality of the performances. As I watched, I realized that it wasn't about the quality of each child's performance but the willingness to perform to one's potential. Schools did auditions not to select for quality but for appropriate content.

Most people in the audience were friends, parents, relatives, and neighbors of the performers. Nobody seemed to mind that routines weren't polished or perfect, even for very poor and rather embarrassing performances. People encouraged each other when parents showed any nervousness about their child's performance. Everyone laughed happily and applauded unreservedly when they were pleased and encouraged each child for doing their best.

I witnessed this again and again at talent shows, spring concerts, and fall concerts. Students did not perform for perfection but for progressive achievement and growth. There was absolutely no competition.

While my two children were in school, my husband and I could go and enjoy these events two to three times a year for about sixteen years, and we never heard any complaints or criticism about the quality of the event. Each time on our way home from an event, we always admired the patience and generosity of all of the adults, both teachers and parents.

One year, it was the night of the talent show in my children's school. Children performed normally, until there was a sudden highlight with a special guest. They introduced Mr. Willow and his band. Mr. Willow was the school janitor and played guitar with his band as a hobby. Children jumped and cheered for him loudly as he made himself a star on that night in the school auditorium. All of the parents enjoyed his band too. I couldn't believe my eyes. Would it be possible in Korea for a school janitor to perform at a *Hakyehoe* no matter how great he is?

To top off the event, the principal and her husband did a polka dance. It was hilarious! To me, it was the best talent show or *Hakyehoe* that I had ever seen in my entire life.

4. My Lies

After I found out my mom was divorced and experienced people's hostile responses towards my fatherlessness, I began to feel stressed when other people asked me about my father. People didn't intend to hurt me by asking, but I couldn't tell the truth anymore because I had learned how others would react and that there would be a change to my relationships. So the question felt like a blow and cornered me each time. I had to do something to guard myself against the question.

My mom and aunts told me that I don't have to tell the truth unnecessarily. It was a harmless suggestion, but they could never know what I went through internally each time I had to lie. I hated lying, but after I pondered and thought of so many different methods to save myself, I also found it to be the only answer. I had to do something to defend myself in order to be able to mingle with people regularly like a normal person. I hated it, but it was better than feeling embarrassed and ashamed again and again. I was determined not to allow people to despise me unnecessarily and chose to disguise myself in the lies. It was self-defense after accumulating so many experiences of people changing their attitude in reaction to my background.

In order to cope with the lying, I convinced myself to believe my lies and made-up truths and trained myself to give the same answer perfectly and without emotion so people could believe me. And any guilt I did feel from lying, I channeled into hatred towards my father, who existed somewhere, because it was his fault I had to lie.

Once I was ready to use it, it was the best invention I came up with to let me survive like a normal person. It also saved many people from being offended and disturbed by my background. The lying worked for both me and others, preventing any hindrances to our growing relationship.

The lie was simply that my father had passed away when I was a baby, so I have no memories of him. He died long ago when I was a baby. I wasn't even one year old. So I don't remember him one bit. He was killed in a car accident. It was very sudden, when he went away on a trip, far away from home. It was a very tragic accident. My mom was very sad. I didn't want to bother her asking about him. I don't remember anything; I was only a baby.

At least part of the lie was true—that I had never seen him nor had any memories of him in my life. My conscience resisted since I didn't actually know if he was still alive or not, but I forced myself not to care.

He didn't even know me either, so why should I worry whether he was dead or alive?

It was the simplest way I knew to quell people's curiosity about my father. I thanked my lie because it truly saved me a countless number of times. And ironically, this lie was better than the truth. People unexpectedly showed me sympathy or compassion for my imaginary dead father. So I played this lie automatically like a recorder every time I was asked about him, for over forty years of my life, as long as I could remember.

In retrospect, it's inconceivable just how many people I met in my life wanted to know about my father. Almost everyone was interested in him. Why? Did people think it was impossible to go through life without a father figure? And some people wanted to know more about him than my prepared scenario. I hated those people. Why did they want to know about somebody's dead dad so much? Once these kinds of people had their curiosity piqued, they were obsessed, out of control. Couldn't they sense or tell when somebody didn't want to keep talking about a sensitive subject?

Once, when I was a sophomore in college, I was on the bus heading home from school. There was a male student on the bus who sat next to me, wanting to talk. He introduced himself as a senior at our school and asked me for my name, major, and what year I was in. Then, he asked me if I would have a cup of coffee with him once we got off the bus. It was the first time we ever met. I laughed it off and asked him if he asks that to every girl he sits next to on the bus. He said no, not at all, and asked if we sat together on the bus next time if I would go for coffee with him then. I thought it was cute, so I said yes without giving it too much thought. I didn't expect to see him again.

But the next week, he sat next to me on the same bus again. As soon as he saw me, he reminded me of my promise. I couldn't think of a reason to refuse and had some free time, so I said okay since it was only coffee.

We got off the bus, and he walked me to a specialty coffee shop a couple of blocks from the bus stop that he was familiar with. Once we entered the shop, he led me to a corner seat in a separate booth. I was shocked to see almost ten of his friends sitting waiting for us there, who began applauding and whistling when we entered. I was puzzled, but I sat there quietly, not knowing what to do with the situation. As soon as I sat down, everyone raised their hands with questions, looking at me. I didn't pick anyone, so they began throwing random questions at me.

The first question hit me like a brick: "What does your father do for a living?"

Still in shock at the situation, I found I couldn't lie.

I thought to myself, *I'd better not show my nervousness.* With a grin, I deflected the question with two words: "Excuse me." I got up gently with a smile and left the seat calmly. I made it look like I was heading towards the lady's room, leaving the booth slowly, but broke into a run as soon as I was out of the shop. I ran and jumped onto a bus that had just arrived at the bus stop.

This happened right before winter break, when I quit school and got married and came to America. I never saw those people again.

I don't know how I survived moments like that. Moments like that with overly inquisitive people would trigger a panic attack: sweating, goosebumps, my heart thumping loudly, dizziness, and a sudden blush on my face. Whoever it was that asked me too many questions, I "blacklisted" and avoided them for a good while.

However, after my born-again experience in 2000, I came to realize that my habitual lying about my father caused me to lie much more than the average person. It was a chain that I needed to break free of, so I began to pray about it.

> *Therefore each of you must put off falsehood and speak truthfully to your neighbor, for we are all members of one body.*
> **Ephesians 4:25**

> *Do not lie to each other, since you have tak-*

en off your old self with its practices and have put on the new self, which is being renewed in knowledge in the image of its Creator.

Colossians 3:9–10

If we confess our sins, he is faithful and just and will forgive us our sins and purify us from all unrighteousness.

1 John 1:9

5. The Gift of God

A decade earlier, in 1989, I remember a conversation I had with my aunt during a sleepover, about a week before I left for America. As we lay in bed, she suddenly asked me something that we had never talked about before. "Do you know your father?"

Shocked, I exclaimed, "What? Oh my goodness, why would you ask me that? Yes, you mean the man who divorced my mom! I read his name on my birth certificate. Didn't he desert both my mom and me? I don't need him." I felt myself getting angry as I spoke, but what she said next left me stunned.

"No, that's not your father. There was somebody else after she got divorced."

Oh my god! "What? Are you serious? I can't believe it! That must be a joke! Unbelievable! Why are you telling me this now? I don't care! I don't have time for this now."

She went on to tell me my biological father's name, which I had never heard or known until then. Apparently, he was married at the time, with children, and he never even knew of my existence.

I tried to look like I didn't care, but there was a tornado of confusion raging inside of me. This was even more horrible than what I had thought was the truth. Not only had my mom and I been deserted; I was a child born out of wedlock. But I was leaving for America within a week; I didn't have any time to think about him further. So I continued to tell myself I didn't care and that the fact that I hated him didn't change anyways.

I am so blessed to have one gorgeous son and one beautiful daughter from God. They are the best gifts and treasures given to me by Him, and I wouldn't change a single thing about them.

My son Richard was my first child, and I was pleased to watch my husband loving him. But when my daughter Ashley was born almost five years later, while I was just as happy to see how my husband loved her, it was a slightly different experience. It was like my eyes were opened, and I was seeing for the first time in my life the love of a father towards his daughter that only a father can give.

It happened one day when my husband was adoring our toddler Ashley in the living room, and I heard her giggling. I gazed at the scene through the kitchen window while I was working and suddenly stopped. Suddenly, I felt new, mixed emotions that I had never felt before. I became lost in thought and feelings when the thought entered my mind, *I wish I were that baby!* I couldn't believe that I was envying her, my baby daughter.

At first, I felt embarrassed. I didn't realize I was feeling envy until that thought. I was just so overwhelmed at seeing the pure love and adoration a father would give his daughter. It was like I could see myself, as a little girl, watching the scene, envious, and I realized what was missing in my own heart. There was a void lacking the love of a father. I had never even known it was missing. I looked into my heart and found a huge void, and I felt a sudden pang and wave of pain surge in my chest.

Silently panicking, I ran to my bathroom and turned on the water in the shower. I burst out crying as my heart ached, sending tremors throughout my body. I missed my father terribly. I couldn't even remember the last time I missed him. I realized that I hadn't allowed myself to miss him since the second grade. I broke down, wailing on the floor, feeling the pain of the little girl in me, who had erased, buried, effaced her father out of her life and didn't allow herself to miss him ever.

Up until that moment, even as an adult, I had never let myself miss my father freely like that. After that first time, I began to miss him more frequently and easily, and I emptied my soul in tears, crying out to God with my pain.

After my mom came to live with me in 1999, I waited patiently for her to open up to me about my father, with what I felt she owed me. I gave her a couple of months to adjust to living with us in a new country. But even after three months, she never said a word and showed no indication of opening up. My anger and frustration grew towards my mom, who had no consideration for her daughter, who had the right to know about her biological father but had only ever been concerned not to hurt her mom.

When I finally demanded to know about my father and for her to apologize for her silence, she was shocked, saying she had never even imagined that I had been agonizing over it.

All she could offer me was a piece of paper of my father's written resume, which she had found in a trash bin. They had happened to stay at the same boarding house for a month while transitioning in their lives: mom from a horrible, short, two-month marriage and divorce, and him from unemployment. They became friends and spent just one night together. Then he left and was gone from her life, never knowing that I was conceived.

Hearing my mom tell me the truth was only more devastating and shocking. I was conceived from a one-night affair, like in a drama or a movie. I was born from two very lost and unwise people who never should have met each other.

It felt like a volcano was erupting inside of me, and I yelled at my mom, "Didn't you know you shouldn't do that? How could you do that? Didn't you know he was married?"

My mom sighed, "I didn't know. I was dumb." *Oh, wow!* Mom sounded so foolish, and her responses only annoyed me further.

I felt myself falling into a dark pit with the endless stream of unanswered questions from my childhood. *Oh God, what an accident I am! Why? Why did You let it be? How could You make me like that? Aren't You God? Wasn't there any other way to make me? Was it the only way? What did I mean to You? Did You know me? Did You want me? Was I even supposed to be born?*

I had asked similar kinds of questions to God millions of times since I was five. Why don't I have a father? Where is he? Why do You want me to live like this without a father? Why can't I have a father? Can I ever see him? Why do I have to live here with my grandmother? Can I live somewhere else? Can I live just with my mom only, without Grandmother?

Two years later, I called my cousin in Korea one

summer day and asked her if she could try to find my biological father using the information from his old resume. At that time, the Internet was booming, and everyone was looking for old friends and family. Inspired by one story after another, I grew curious and decided to take a chance, even though it seemed unlikely. I wasn't expecting much.

But in less than two weeks, my cousin called back with his cell phone number. My head spun as I looked at the number. It was another bet with nothing to lose.

My mom and I set a time to call him after dinner when nobody else was home. We sat quietly in the kitchen, taking deep breaths, and I pressed the numbers with a prayer. I told myself it was only a fifty-fifty chance.

As the phone rang, I felt myself becoming dizzy and short of breath, like I was riding a roller coaster and slowly reaching the peak. *Oh God, help me!* After only a few rings, a real man far on the other side of the ocean answered.

I spoke quickly as if grasping for him, "Hello! Is your name OOO, sir?"

"Yes, I am." *Oh, God! This must be him!* I took a deep breath and recited my prepared speech.

"Sir, I'm calling from America. My name is OOO. Please do not be alarmed. Please do not hang up. You don't know me. But I had to call you to find out if you were real and that you existed. Do you remember OOO? That's my mom. She told me that she lived in this region in the late '60s, and that you are my father." Then, I was silent. I had no thoughts left.

There was a pause. Then, he murmured, "I'm on a train right now. It's hard to talk to you. Can you call me back in an hour?" His voice seemed strained.

"Okay, I will call you back. Thank you, sir." I breathed deeply again after hanging up. Thank God he didn't deny the information or hang up on me. I felt a glimmer of hope.

It was the longest hour ever. I felt anxious, and Mom and I couldn't speak. We just kept watching the clock, filling the hour with our waiting.

An hour and ten minutes passed, and I finally called him back while sitting at my kitchen table. I didn't have to give him my introduction again, so I said hello and then my name. He said that I didn't sound like a spam call or anything when I called him earlier, that I sounded serious enough to make him think about the information. Then, he asked if he could talk to my mom if she was available. I handed the phone to her, and as soon as she answered him, they exchanged a greeting of "How on earth!" The phone wasn't on speaker, but I could hear his voice. My mom explained how I was born, and he repeated "Unbelievable!" again and again. The conversation continued, and they sounded like old friends exchanging old and new memories together. It was the first time my mom had ever spoken to him since the night they shared.

After they finished talking, it was finally my turn to talk to him, finally, after thirty-two years. He admitted to me that I must be from him, from that one night with my mom. He said this was the most overwhelming thing in his life. He said that he was my biological father, and he was so sorry for his absence in my life. He thanked me for supporting my mom and told me that I must be a good daughter. Every word he spoke to me sounded like it was coming from his heart, and I could perceive and feel his kindness.

I thanked God and thanked my father again and again for acknowledging me, not denying me, and that's all I needed. I had one more paragraph prepared for him, saying that the purpose of this call was completely pure. There was nothing more I wanted from him than to hear his voice. I respected him and his family, so I would never harm him and his family with my presence. I assured him there was nothing to worry about.

He told me that I had three half-siblings and kindly asked me if I wanted to be introduced. But I knew Korean culture and that I would not be welcomed by them. I didn't want to make them uncomfortable by my presence. I knew I should not be selfish but wise. I thanked him, but I told him that this was enough and that I would just like to talk to him again if I could.

And as we conversed, I pressed the phone against my ear with both hands and closed my eyes, intentionally absorbing every single word he spoke to me. I trembled with delight and was choking in tears; I didn't want to miss a single word, and I soaked my senses with his voice. Everything he said soothed me, and I felt like a weight was lifted from my soul, which was coming alive. I felt like I was melting to the ground as my tears of joy flowed down my face. I thanked my ears for hearing his voice.

There was something very new but somehow familiar, this melting in my soul, which I had never felt with my mom. My mom had always made me wonder how I resembled her or what I inherited from her. But this experience through a short phone conversation made me feel overwhelmingly delighted. It satisfied my soul.

It was the gift of God that night to be connected to my biological father. We exchanged pages and pages of personal letters with pictures through the mail, and he told me so much about his life. We talked about five or six more times on the phone, and each time, it was like thirty minutes of heaven.

Hearing his voice was a completely different experience from anything else. I didn't have a hard time talking with him, as I did with my husband or my mom. Even though we couldn't see each other, we just understood each other without needing any explanations. It was the first time I ever felt so fully understood and adored by another person in the world.

I grew an overflowing desire to run out to Korea

and meet him in person right away. I wanted to see him with my own eyes and feel him in my arms. But much to my dismay, my circumstances at the time wouldn't allow me to do that. I was working almost full time, and no one in the house could help me either. My mom was completely dependent on me, my husband neglected and avoided me, and my young children demanded of me every day.

But money was the real problem. I couldn't afford an airline ticket to go to Korea. I had paid a couple grand for an attorney's fee to help file for my mom's green card and all of her other needs, including out-of-pocket doctor expenses since we didn't have health insurance then. I worked hard all the time to provide for everyone else, but I never had any money left over for myself. Also, I remembered that my purpose in calling my father was just to find him and not to disturb his life. I wet my pillow with tears many nights in agony over this.

On the fifth or sixth phone call over a couple of months, I heard a sudden disturbance in my father's voice, and he said, "Sorry to end the call with you so abruptly," and hung up.

I called him a few days later, but the phone number was no longer in service. He could have called me, but he never did. I tried calling him again and again, but it was the same thing. So that was the end of our phone rendezvous.

I am grateful that I was given the chance to share

my faith with him, telling him about Jesus and salvation and emphasizing that that's all I wanted for him so that I could see him in heaven.

> *For God so loved the world that he gave his one and only Son, that whoever believes in him shall not perish but have eternal life. For God did not send his Son into the world to condemn the world, but to save the world through him. Whoever believes in him is not condemned, but whoever does not believe stands condemned already because they have not believed in the name of God's one and only Son.*
>
> **John 3:16–18**

It was the late fall of 2017. My church is a multi-cultural church, so every couple of Sundays a month, we have Scripture read by members of the congregation in another language. I participate in this once or twice a year, reading a verse in Korean and in English.

I received an email with the assigned verse and schedule, and I was delighted because the verse was a popular one and also one of my favorites, which I recite to myself frequently.

> *So do not fear, for I am with you; do not be dismayed, for I am your God. I will strengthen you and help you; I will uphold you with my righteous right hand.*

Isaiah 41:10

However, the assignment included one more verse before it, so it was Isaiah 41:9–10. I couldn't remember verse 9, so I hurriedly grabbed my Bible and flipped through the pages. It blew me away as I read it.

> *I took you from the ends of the earth, from its farthest corners I called you. I said, "You are my servant"; I have chosen you and have not rejected you.*
>
> **Isaiah 41:9**

As I read the verse, I heard God's voice like thunder in my head and my heart. His voice echoed and shook my body and soul: *I took you from the ends of the earth, from the very edge, never refused, but intended for you!*

He allowed me, He meant for me, and He chose me, in that particular way, to be His servant, for His special purpose! This message drenched my soul and satisfied my being. Thank you, God!

My God has been right next to me at every moment of my life. He has never left me once. Through my writing, line by line, He has shown me that He was right there beside me, watching over me.

I don't know if or how much my story will bless other people, yet it has blessed me. I'm being carried through and soaked in His love. This writing has provided special time for me to spend with my Father. I found Him where I had not seen Him before, in every corner of my life, like a game of hide and seek.

God has unfolded my story, bringing me places in my memories and showing me what I missed. With His tender sweetness and comfort, I was found by Him as His child and a new creation. God is more than enough; His way is perfect!

As for God, his way is perfect: The LORD's word is flawless; he shields all who take refuge in him.
Psalm 18:30

But now, this is what the LORD says—he who created you, Jacob, he who formed you, Israel: "Do not fear, for I have redeemed you; I have summoned you by name; you are mine."
Isaiah 43:1

I will say to the north, "Give them up!" and to the south, "Do not hold them back." Bring my sons from afar and my daughters from the ends of the earth—everyone who is called by my name, whom I created for my glory, whom I formed and made.
Isaiah 43:6–7

Remember these things, Jacob, for you, Israel, are my servant. I have made you, you are my servant; Israel, I will not forget you.
Isaiah 44:21

"For I know the plans I have for you," declares the LORD, "plans to prosper you and not to harm you, plans to give you hope and a future."

Jeremiah 29:11

My Mom & I

But he knows the way that I take; when he has tested me, I will come forth as gold.

Job 23:10

May your father and mother rejoice; may she who gave you birth be joyful!

Proverbs 23:25

Children, obey your parents in the Lord, for this is right. "Honor your father and mother"—which is the first commandment with a promise—"so that it may go well with you and that you may enjoy long life on the earth." Fathers, do not exasperate your children; instead, bring them up in the training and instruction of the Lord.

Ephesians 6:1–4

1. My Mom's Young Daughter

Whenever I had to discipline my young children, my mom would always interrupt me. I pleaded with her to not interrupt me many times, but it was no use.

She said the same thing every time: "When your

mom was little, she never caused any trouble. I didn't have to do much for her. I didn't have to worry about her because she never caused any problems. I never had to correct her or yell at her. She was the one who worried about me. She always let me know where she played. She always did her job well. I didn't ever have to raise my voice. She grew up by herself. It was so easy to raise her." I would stop her from scolding my children like this, but her rants made me start thinking about myself.

I realized that I couldn't easily recall anything from my childhood. Once I started college, I tried my best to erase all of my childhood memories because there was nothing I wanted to remember. Remembering my childhood always brought pain along with it.

Once I became a mother, there was nothing more important to me than raising my children, even if it was so difficult for me. I felt like I needed to understand my children better as they grew older, so I couldn't avoid revisiting my past. I couldn't just go back once; I had to keep going back to learn. I wanted to know what I was thinking at their age, what I did or didn't like about myself, how I wanted my mom to act, and so on.

I looked back in my memories, and I saw myself as a young girl around the age of six or seven, playing on a narrow, slopy road filled with children since there wasn't anywhere else to play. I saw the girl running back and forth between her friends and her mom, letting her know where she was going each hour. Her mom never had to go out and search for her daughter because she always told her mom where she would be.

A few years later, the girl is a little older, around eight or nine years old. She's running with a backpack and a paper in her hand. She is so excited to show it to her mom. When Mom's eyes open wide with excitement and a grin spreads on her face like a rainbow, the girl begins jumping with joy that she made her mom so happy. She's determined to bring home more certificates to make Mom happy.

Every day after school, the girl would tell her mom about her day, from the minute she left home to the minute she returned. She loved to give Mom a report of her day like a diary entry, and it was her way of entertaining her. And anytime she learned something new at school, she would show it to her mom. Mom didn't graduate from elementary school due to her illness, so the girl wanted to share her experiences. If she learned a new song, she sang it for Mom. If she heard a story, she acted it out like she was on stage. She told Mom about the Earth and solar system and how the Earth is tilted at 23.5 degrees, which causes seasons, all drawn out on paper.

The girl was bullied by her classmates sometimes

because her mom was hunchbacked. Even though it wasn't true, it made her cry and be afraid to look at her mom's back. And there were times when she was even mistreated by some teachers at school, but she didn't tell her mom about it because she knew it would only make her upset. It pained me to see this younger version of myself in my recollections.

When the girl started watching American TV shows in the fifth grade, she learned about showing affection to family members, like kissing, hugging, or saying "I love you." This was extremely uncommon in Korean culture, even for parents, but it gave her the idea that Mom needed love because she seemed to be the loneliest in her eyes. The girl showed love to her mom every morning and night through kisses, hugs, and saying "I love you," even if she didn't receive anything in return. Her mom always answered her daughter only with, "Me too!" The girl continued this tradition for many years.

As she was growing up, she gladly volunteered to help Mom with some chores at home, although she didn't like doing them. She couldn't help but worry about her feeble mom at home all day, especially while she was home with her grandmother. It was hard to concentrate on her schoolwork sometimes because of this.

Another couple of years later, in high school, the girl came back home from the movies one day, which was rare. She tried to explain the movie *Terminator*, but she had to explain the meaning of the word "terminator," along with the genre of science fiction, technology, and other American ideas. She began to feel exasperated and wanted to give up.

One day she used a saved coin to call Mom during her lunch break. There was only one public phone at school, next to the teachers' office in the main lobby, which was in the other wing. But it didn't matter how far it was from her classroom. When she called home, Mom was very happily surprised. So she kept saving coins to call Mom once a day, even during short breaks between classes. She did this from elementary school all the way to high school. Later, when she began commuting to college in another city, long-distance calling was expensive, but she still called once or twice a week.

Recalling all of these childhood memories didn't help and only overwhelmed me. I remembered clearly how much empathy I had for my mom, so it was saddening that my children never seemed to empathize with me. It perplexed and confused me for a while because my children, compared to the younger me, were beginning to look bad. Obviously, they didn't seem to understand or care about my complaints at all. Later on, I realized that they didn't have to understand me because their mom wasn't like their grandmother, the mom I had when I was a child.

I also was forced to remember what I had taught my children with emphasis: they shouldn't worry about me, their mom. Even now, I remind them that they should enjoy whatever they want to do without worrying about me; that's what makes their mom happy.

A few years ago, I went to a theater by myself. It was a good, rare escape from a stressful day. There was this dialogue between a mom and her teenage daughter: the daughter told her mom to be careful and that she was worried for her, but the mother looked straight into her eyes and told her, "Don't worry about your mom. Being worried is for moms, not for children!" When I heard that line, I burst into tears and sobbed for a while. For the first time in my life, I wished that my mom could've told me that! For the first time, I thought about asking her, "Did you like that your daughter worried about you all the time?"

2. A Pledge with The Prince of Egypt

As soon as my husband and I came to America in 1989, I began praying for my mom to come and live with us. I prayed for ten years.

Growing up, people told me that I'd have to support my mom. I didn't have any issues with this. One of the major teachings of Confucianism is to be good to your parents, and so I, as an only child, had to take care of my mom. Moreover, I had watched her suffer from my grandmother, which compelled me to rescue her. And lastly, I loved my mom more than anything in the world.

Meanwhile, in America, my two precious children were growing up so fast, and I felt bad that they didn't know their grandma — their mom's mom. My children prayed with me for her arrival, but it felt as though no matter how hard I prayed, God wasn't hearing me. After I received the news of her second visa rejection, I began to lose hope that God would give my mom a better life away from my grandmother. I had never let go of that dream before, even while growing up. But I'd never heard of anyone from South Korea being rejected. I began to grow bitter as I watched more and more new people arrive every week at my Korean church.

I became angry with God, and I felt too bitter to pray. I felt like I was losing my mind. When I did pray, my prayers were rebellious. I yelled in my car, "I don't like You, God! I hate You! How can You do this to me? What have I done wrong? Don't You think it would be better for my mom to come here? Why won't You grant this for us? Why? I might as well stop praying; You aren't listening to me anyway. Why should I bother? Why?"

A couple of months after my bitterness took over, a new animated movie called *The Prince of Egypt* came out. Ashley was three years old at the time, and we hadn't been to the theater in a while, but I thought it would be good for my son, Richard, who was now seven. My husband and I decided we would take turns watching Ashley, who was a really wild toddler in the lobby. But as soon as we got in the theater, she fell asleep in her stroller, and we all got to enjoy the movie sitting together side by side. I normally didn't get any leisure time, so I was especially pleased and let myself become engrossed in the story.

It was about a well-known Bible story of Moses bringing the Israelites out of Egypt.[1] When the narrator began introducing the story, I was instantly hooked: they were Israelites; they were God's hand-picked, chosen people. But they were in slavery, far from their homes, for over four hundred years. They cried out to God to free them. But God didn't listen. They cried out more. But God didn't answer. God seemed cold and distant from them. People were born as slaves. They died as slaves. They had no choice but to wait. It wasn't time for God to fulfill His plan yet.

Moses fled to the desert, running desperately for his life, even though he was a prince of Egypt, because he murdered an Egyptian in rage, which was not by God's will. He had to hide in the wilderness, hopelessly, watching flocks of sheep as a shepherd. He lived an ordinary life, waiting for God, for forty years until the king of Egypt and that generation passed away. Everything was moving so slowly but, at the same time, was

---

1 Moses' story is history and can be found in Exodus, the second book of the Bible.

rushing towards God's perfect timing.

Finally, God called upon Moses. It was His time. Everything had to be according to His time and will. Because it was the plan made by God from the beginning. He was watching everything and everyone from the beginning of time. Men were given free will as God's creation, but they were living on their own, rejecting God. Pharaoh resisted letting the Israelites go until his beloved son died, and when God's time came, there was nothing that could stop Him.

God is so *big*. I knew He was the creator of heaven and earth, but God's portrayal in this movie was beyond my perception. He couldn't be contained by me or my thoughts.

What am I? I felt so tiny, not even casting a shadow. And God didn't owe me anything.

What have I done! I dared to control and blame God. I trembled in fear. I saw the lost and rebellious child in me being reflected vividly on the screen.

Who am I? I'm not an Israelite. I'm not part of God's chosen people. I'm just a gentile. My ancestors worshipped other gods. They didn't know God at all and persecuted those who did worship Him. I am a gentile, far from God's people. But still, I'm chosen. How could this be possible? It is because of Jesus, through His sacrifice for me. I am saved by Jesus! I was chosen by grace! But what did I do? I rebelled. I sinned against God.

This realization hit me hard, in my head and my heart. I shook. Ashley slept through the movie for the first time at a theater. I had not watched an entire movie from start to finish since she was born. It was the strangest thing that I could watch it in complete comfort, as if I had to watch it thoroughly, with no disturbances. I felt exhausted in my mind. In my heart, I was convinced that I had sinned against God because of my recent rebellion.

The next morning, it was unusually quiet. My husband left for work, Richard went to school, Ashley fell asleep for an early nap, and I had the day off. It was like it was planned.

I couldn't escape my thoughts from the movie last night. Still trembling in awe of God, I fell onto the floor, prostrate before Him. Crying out, I repented. *I'm sorry, Almighty God! I was terrible. Forgive me, please, God! Who am I? I'm nothing, nobody! You don't have to grant my prayer if it is not Your will. You don't have to do anything for me, even if I want it badly. You know better. I don't care about my mom coming or not coming anymore because You know better. You don't have to answer that. But if she comes, I promise I will support her until You take her away. I pledge that I will do my best to take care of her until the last day of her life. Only if it is Your will, and Your will will be done! Whatever You do, I don't care. Thank You, God! Thank You, my Father!*

It was my sincerest prayer. That was February

1999. I became relieved and felt set free of the burden of bringing my mom here. I didn't worry about it anymore and nearly forgot all about it. It was the first time I felt such peace.

I remember there was one song I hated so much in my youth. "I've got peace like a river. I've got peace like a river. I've got peace like a river in my soul. Hallelujah!" Then the second verse repeated with "joy," and so on. I was in about fifth grade, spending my Saturdays in the children's program at the Catholic church, and they had us sing this song frequently. It was so long. It killed me because my circumstances were anything but peaceful, and I didn't really know what peace was.

In May, my mom called me and said she was coming in June.

For he chose us in him before the creation of the world to be holy and blameless in his sight. In love he predestined us for adoption to sonship through Jesus Christ, in accordance with his pleasure and will—to the praise of his glorious grace, which he has freely given us in the One he loves.

Ephesians 1:4–6

3. A New Trial

Some people at Newark airport applauded as I

ran from a distance crying out "Umma, Umma!"[2] and hugged my mom. It would have been quite the news story: the meeting of a mother and daughter parted by the seas for over a decade.

My mom arrived in Newark, New Jersey, in June 1999 and came to my home.

My mom was an angel in my memories, so I thought living with her would be easy, like a happily ever after. I was confident that I could make her happy.

But as reality unfolded, it felt like I was thrown into a survival scene from a thriller mystery movie. I'm not trying to exaggerate or complain, but to describe the struggle of living with my mom and being married to my husband is challenging. I could never have put it into words at the time. It was suffocating, being trapped between two people who were so different and who kept bringing their conflicts to such a simple person like myself. They were like oil and water.

Additionally, I never realized just how tight our living space was until my mom came. For years, my daughter Ashley, often wishing for her own space, had to share her room with her grandmother. We didn't have any private spaces in the house for my mom, but she also didn't try to give us any space. She was always home with nowhere to go, 24/7, 365 days a year, like a sheet of music on repeat.

---

2 Mom in Korean, pronounced "uhm-ma."

Some of my relatives and Korean friends were so jealous when they heard that my mom was living with me. They thought that my mom was spoiling me and that I was living like a princess. Some even thought that my mom was rich. They all looked so confident saying these things that I was too embarrassed to tell them that my mom is weak, handicapped, penniless, and fully dependent on me.

When most people think of their elderly mothers or grandmothers, they imagine wise and gentle women whom they could turn to for life advice or to share their joys and struggles. But that was not my mother.

Sandwiched

When my mom first arrived, my husband immediately developed an attitude. The air between my mom and husband was thick to the point that I couldn't breathe being in the same room with them. There wasn't a moment where he wasn't tense and irritated at my mom.

Maybe they didn't get along because of my mom's awkward, dry personality. To be fair, even from my point of view, my mom was extremely odd, timid, and sometimes senseless, appearing like a child rather than an adult. She wasn't anything like *his* mother, who was overly confident, boasted frequently, and took control of situations. On top of that, she wasn't anything like a typical Korean mother-in-law either. Culturally, Korean mothers-in-law are expected to pamper their sons-in-law with cooking and care, but my mom couldn't provide any of those things. Instead of spoiling her son-in-law, she was more like a lost child in the middle of our family. She would follow after me asking, "What do you want me to do?"

But while I could understand if all of this was greatly disappointing to him, I couldn't accept it as his rightful reason to be unfriendly. He was noticeably unfriendly to her, and it caused me mental strain beyond measure.

I wanted to fix the situation so badly, and I tried to mend the broken relationship between them. I hated seeing two people who I cared about being so distant from one another, but I was so squished. It felt like I was being sandwiched between the two of them! I went back and forth to each of them, pleading and persuading my husband to be nice to my mom while trying to explain my husband's attitude to her. And in front of my mom, with all my strength, I acted like everything was normal because I've always protected her and worried about her. But on the inside, I was devastated, as my heart was broken.

My husband didn't do anything that he promised he would do for my mom before she came. Since God didn't give me the ability to discern people's intentions and made me as simple as I am, I couldn't understand why my husband—*my life partner*—was giving me such a hard time for what should have been the happiest time of my life with my mom joining us.

His betrayal traumatized me. My disappointment in him started to spiral out of control. He seemed so immature, and I started to think about divorce more seriously. For more than a decade, I continually debated in my mind with whom I was supposed to live: my mom or my husband? I asked God a million times, but He didn't answer me.

In 2012, during my annual fast in January, God spoke to me through the book of Jeremiah, chapters 42–43. When I read the part where the people of the land petitioned the Prophet Jeremiah to pray to God about whether they should stay or leave, I felt myself in their shoes, asking God a similar question. Then, I received the crystal clear answer "to stay in my marriage," and that "God would bless me and my family through it."

When the Prophet Jeremiah delivered the message of God to the petitioners to stay where they were, I said, "Amen." But to my shock, the petitioners who had convinced me to pledge with them in the scriptures by saying, "I will obey God whether I like it or not!" (Jeremiah 42:6), became outraged against the message Jeremiah delivered, now saying, "It's a lie!" Their proud flesh could not agree with God. Consequently, the people moved where they were told not to go and were destroyed. I will say, fasting made me humble and gave me the strength to do God's will.

Each time I died to my pride and righteousness, my faithful God lifted me up and enabled me to do one thing at a time, supporting me fully and invisibly, making impossible things possible (Matthew 19:26, 2 Corinthians 12:9, Philippians 4:13). Surely, He protected my entire family, providing for us beyond my imagination, even when I felt like a flattened sandwich between my husband and my mom.

No matter how much I had suffered, I was able to forgive my husband through the grace of God. From the bottom of my heart, I thank him all the way to eternity for everything he endures living with my mom. I love him with a new God-given perspective. I know no average man could do what he has done, letting his mother-in-law live with him in the same house for twenty years, from the beginning of our marriage until now, while supporting us all financially and providing a loving home for us. Who can beat that?

> *Jesus looked at them and said, "With man this is impossible, but with God all things are possible."*
> **Matthew 19:26**

> *I can do all this through him who gives me strength.*
> **Philippians 4:13**

When they hurled their insults at him, he did not retaliate; when he suffered, he made no threats. Instead, he entrusted himself to him who judges justly. "He himself bore our sins" in his body on the cross, so that we might die to sins and live for righteousness; "by his wounds you have been healed."

1 Peter 2:23–24

Three times I pleaded with the Lord to take it away from me. But he said to me, "My grace is sufficient for you, for my power is made perfect in weakness." Therefore I will boast all the more gladly about my weaknesses, so that Christ's power may rest on me.

2 Corinthians 12:8–9

Get rid of all bitterness, rage, and anger, brawling, and slander, along with every form of malice. Be kind and compassionate to one another, forgiving each other, just as in Christ God forgave you.

Ephesians 4:31–32

At the same time, there were also conflicts occurring between my mom and my children. This happened in the first month, only a couple of weeks after my mom arrived.

When I called my mom from work, she was upset at Richard for something that must have been a communication issue, and nobody knew exactly what it was. At the time, I had to be fair to both of them since I was far away at work, but I must have leaned towards my mom's side more because she just came from Korea and wasn't used to living with us. I asked Richard to apologize to his grandma. He refused and told me that he didn't do anything wrong. My mom got even more upset and started saying how rude her grandson was. I was stuck at work and needed to find a way to resolve the situation as quickly as possible. Getting stressed, I demanded Richard to apologize immediately, or I would send him to Korea. But my stubborn almost-eight-year-old son was feeling righteous and continued to insist that he did absolutely nothing wrong and would go to Korea instead. What could I say? I ended up telling him to pack up and that I would take him to the airport when I got home.

As soon as I walked through the front door, there was nothing but chaos. Ashley, who had just turned three, was crying so hard that her eyes were swollen shut. Richard was ready to leave with his luggage packed at the door, and she really believed her brother was leaving. My mom did nothing to de-escalate the situation for all those hours.

I quickly took Ashley to the corner to calm her down, and I whispered in her ear, "I'm sorry, my baby! Mommy promises you; I will bring Richard back soon. Trust me, don't worry!" As I met her eyes with a warm smile, little Ashley looked at me trustingly and nodded.

After I finished comforting Ashley, I took Richard out of the house to talk to him. He came out with his luggage and asked, "Don't I have to purchase an airline ticket first? Where's my passport?" I took him to my car and drove him around. I told him about Grandma's harsh life so he would have some empathy for his grandma, which brought him peace. We drove home, and he apologized to her.

It was an exhausting day for me, and I think it was the best I could've done for everyone. I thanked God that my husband wasn't home that day.

Throughout the years of raising my children, I taught them to be empathetic and respectful to their grandma. I encouraged them to apologize to her first whenever conflict occurred. This wasn't only because of my mom's background, but it was also because of Korean culture. Holding high respect for elders was very important, and it was the way that my mom had lived her life.

However, my children were growing up in America, and they didn't like compromising their beliefs when the matter was about fairness. There was both a cultural gap and also a thick language barrier between my children and my mom. Sometimes cultural cues conflicted. For example, I rebuked my son for looking into my eyes intently when I was angry, which is rude in Korean culture. Then he reminded me, "Didn't you say that I have to look at someone's eyes when they're talking to me?" He would continually ask me throughout the years, "Is this a time I should look at your eyes or not?" And their grandma didn't understand even the slightest bit of English.

I frequently had to arbitrate between my children and their grandmother whenever there was conflict between them. I wondered if there would ever come a day when they could resolve their own conflicts. But I could never just leave it up to my mom because she hadn't achieved or developed her own strategies for communication. She was completely dependent on me to mediate between them every single time, so I never skipped resolving an issue. At the same time, any kind of conflict also stressed me greatly. Perhaps that is one of my problems caused by my youth growing up with my own grandmother, that I can't stand conflict or tension in the air.

This is the Bible verse I used to emphasize to my children to care for and honor their grandmother: "Truly I tell you, whatever you did for one of the least of these brothers and sisters of mine, you did for me" (Matthew 25:40).

It might sound strange that I used this verse, asking my children to consider their grandmother as the least, but in my eyes, there was no one poorer than my mom from childhood. So they came to understand that their needy grandmother was not like other grandmothers they met at church that lived independently. And they could see that I provided everything for her, just like a needy child. We all lived together, so there was no way I could hide it.

On top of resolving conflicts for my mom, I began to resume all of the comforting entertainment I provided for her as a child. But as an adult, my means became more limited: I obviously wasn't going to sing, dance, and put on shows for her anymore, so we just talked. My life turned back to the days where I would report my daily routines and events to her after school, except now it was after work. I spent almost two hours every day, even after my long and hard work, even while raising two children.

I had to; otherwise, my poor mom would be so lonely with no other adults to talk to. I definitely talked to her more than to my husband, which was okay because he didn't like it when I talked too much anyway. Moreover, my mom needed daily education on basic life skills to live with us smoothly. Although she helped me watch the children while I worked, more of my energy was being consumed by her as if I was raising yet another child.

When my mom came to live with us, she was sixty years old. She couldn't handle anything without a list of instructions, so I still cooked on my days off to put meals in the fridge. And when I worked, I called her at least twice during the day.

However, I must say that as my children were

growing, they helped me help their grandmother more than I expected them to. Sometimes they took better care of her than I did and blessed their grandmother.

After I matured more spiritually, I began to perceive all of the spiritual warfare we were up against. And although we didn't know what we were doing, God has never left us nor forsaken us (Deuteronomy 31:8).

We are hard pressed on every side, but not crushed; perplexed, but not in despair; persecuted, but not abandoned; struck down, but not destroyed.

2 Corinthians 4:8–9

For though we live in the world, we do not wage war as the world does. The weapons we fight with are not the weapons of the world. On the contrary, they have divine power to demolish strongholds.

2 Corinthians 10:3–4

My Mom's Mission

Faith had always been a priority for my mom since living her life wouldn't have been possible without faith. We confirmed to each other that we are saved by grace through Jesus's holy blood.

Despite this, only a few days after she came, she

surprised me by saying, "If we are saved, there is nothing more important than keeping the seventh day holy for the Sabbath. That's what God said!"

What I didn't know was that she had started attending a new church that I didn't know about after I left for America. This church preached about keeping laws instead of being grateful for God's grace. It was an empty religion that lacked a personal relationship with Jesus Christ. For the past twenty years, my mom's resolute mission was to convert me to her religion of heresy.

From then on, she criticized me at any given moment by emphasizing how important it is to keep laws if we are saved. Whenever I relaxed and let my guard down, she would suddenly start lecturing me. She would talk about what's prohibited in the Old Testament, especially when I was cooking meat that she doesn't eat, like pork or shrimp.

To me, she sounded like the Pharisees, legalists who were never satisfied and didn't know grace. My heart ached while listening to her flawed lectures, and I gave in to my anger because her theories subverted all that Jesus has done for us.

What I longed to hear from my mom as my senior believer was encouragement or approval of me for my unwavering faith and for my faithful living as her daughter. Instead, I had to hear her erroneous reproaches, which I never imagined I would hear from her. This scary twist and her relentless obstinacy stressed me beyond words.

I knew she had nobody but me, so it made me feel guilty that I couldn't listen to her. In all of my life, I've never seen anyone who lives like my mom. She has no social life. As a pessimist, it doesn't seem to bother her, or maybe her disappointment with people reinforces her pessimism.

At times, it was painful for me to observe my mom's life. So I prayed and offered to help her find some friends, but she always refused. Perhaps *I* was more desperate for her to make friends so that I could be free of the burden of being "everyone" for my mom. Nobody lives like my mom, but no daughter lives like this either. Sometimes I wished I could just be her daughter instead of her caretaker.

This was a new type of burden for me. While I wanted to love the Lord more and live the life He wanted me to live, the pressure that my mom was causing me was testing my patience. In the middle of my distress, God made me remember my *pledge* for my mom, the one I had made the day after watching *The Prince of Egypt*.

Throughout the years, I invited Korean pastors, elders, and Bible school teachers, all to talk to my mom. But one by one, they all shook their heads and left. They agreed to an old Korean proverb: talking with her is like throwing an egg at a rock. Even though my mom didn't graduate from elementary school, I didn't believe my mom was limited. The reason I believed in her was because I believed, deep in my heart, in her desire to be her best. I believed that her potential in her personality and virtue would be realized someday.

I wanted her to understand! She didn't have to worry about keeping all these laws. She just needed to believe that Jesus knows everything she goes through. We are blessed to have Jesus. I wanted her to enjoy what she could and to share the love with whoever God brought to us. *Mom, let's live happily for this day with a grateful heart!*

A few years ago, I invited several American friends from my church to pray for my mom and her salvation. Upon my translation of our prayers, she admitted that she was a sinner and that she believed that Jesus, the Son of God, died on the cross for her sins and rose again. She also acknowledged Him as her Savior confidently. Thank God! Mom loves the Lord and has immovable faith! Every one of my friends and I were convinced of her salvation that day.

Praise God! It was a blessed day from God. I needed that confirmation for my beloved mom, and I was so relieved at her salvation. My mission was accomplished for my mom.

Jesus answered, "I am the way and the truth and the life. No one comes to the Father except

through me."

John 14:6

This righteousness is given through faith in Jesus Christ to all who believe. There is no difference between Jew and Gentile, for all have sinned and fall short of the glory of God, and all are justified freely by his grace through the redemption that came by Christ Jesus.

Romans 3:22–24

If you declare with your mouth, "Jesus is Lord," and believe in your heart that God raised him from the dead, you will be saved. For it is with your heart that you believe and are justified, and it is with your mouth that you profess your faith and are saved.

Romans 10:9–10

It is true that some preach Christ out of envy and rivalry, but others out of goodwill. The latter do so out of love, knowing that I am put here for the defense of the gospel. The former preach Christ out of selfish ambition, not sincerely, supposing that they can stir up trouble for me while I am in chains. But what does it matter? The important thing is that in every way, whether from false motives or true, Christ is preached. And because of this I rejoice.

Philippians 1:15–18

Therefore do not let anyone judge you by what you eat or drink, or with regard to a religious festival, a New Moon celebration or a Sabbath day.

Colossians 2:16

A Journey's End

Twenty years later, I can conclude my story about living with my mom as a journey of discovery. It's like I was wandering in a maze about the mom of my memories while I was living with her, not perceiving who she really is.

I realized that the reason it took so long to figure her out is because I met my mom *as an adult* for the first time. Our reunion occurred over a decade after leaving her in Korea (at the age of twenty-one, in the middle of college) and skipped past my twenties, my marriage, and my journey to a new country.

I suffered through the first decade of living with my mom as an infant Christian, without any knowledge or awareness of spiritual warfare. After the first ten years, I finally acknowledged that my mom and my husband are my God-given missions.

I know now why I suffered so much, other than because of my husband; God showed me the answers. Over the years, two things became very clear: first was my own guilt, that I couldn't make my mom happy no matter what I did, and it hurt me whenever I saw her depressed look. I was only flesh, falling short all the time as an immature believer. But in 2017, the ugly spirit of guilt disappeared from me immediately through group prayer. The other answer was my mom's self-righteousness and self-pity, coming from her victim mindset, even though she loves the Lord! Nevertheless, I believe the day will come (and it's much closer now!) when my mom will be set free from all of her emotional chains.

No matter how she has been, *one thing* I know clearly from the beginning of my life is that *God entrusted her to me.*

The phrase "My mom and I" to me now means "victory" because God has transformed us over the past twenty, long years. There was suffering and complaining as normal human beings, but God turned it around into a story of victory with His wisdom and non-stop love. In the end, I was able to overcome my defeats and enter an amazing new life.

> *No, in all these things we are more than conquerors through him who loved us.*
> **Romans 8:37**

> *No temptation has overtaken you except what is common to mankind. And God is faithful; he will not let you be tempted beyond what you can bear. But when you are tempted, he will also provide a way out so that you can endure it.*

1 Corinthians 10:13

4. Seasons of Struggles

This is a seasonal journal of my human struggle through living with my mom. It shows closely how my spiritual warfare was real.

I do not understand what I do. For what I want to do I do not do, but what I hate I do. And if I do what I do not want to do, I agree that the law is good. As it is, it is no longer I myself who do it, but it is sin living in me. For I know that good itself does not dwell in me, that is, in my sinful nature. For I have the desire to do what is good, but I can not carry it out.

Romans 7:15–18

What a wretched man I am! Who will rescue me from this body that is subject to death? Thanks be to God, who delivers me through Jesus Christ our Lord! So then, I myself in my mind am a slave to God's law, but in my sinful nature a slave to the law of sin.

Romans 7:24–25

My Mom's Life Setting

Living as a shut-in is the setting for my mom's entire life. She is handicapped with upper thoracic curvature, which means her spine is curved toward her inner body. She has lived with this condition since age eleven. It developed during the Korean War when a fever arose from a deadly infection in her spine caused by a swing injury that had occurred three years prior. There was poor treatment during wartime, regardless of how much my grandparents wanted to cure her.

It must have been petrifying to a young child to face possible death, or at best, to be handicapped. She barely survived the fatal illness, not even making full growth during puberty. At age eleven, she was paralyzed for several years but miraculously learned to walk later on in life. A major side effect of her illness is a weak stomach, which is why she has poor digestion and cannot bear any type of motion. Doctors say these could be symptoms or after-effects from the injury.

Therefore, my mom's motion sickness is another cause for her to live as a shut-in, and I have never heard of anybody worse than her. She should be in *Guinness World Records* for having the worst case of motion sickness. That is why she cannot tolerate a car ride at all, not even for five minutes. The top brands of motion sickness medicine barely work. Plus, they still don't prevent my mom from throwing up, and they cause adverse side effects.

We have always hated any kind of doctor's visits. Every doctor's visit is challenging. Every doctor's visit promises vomiting in the car. Each time we arrive at the doctor's office, she exhibits a deadly pallor; no doctor can help her with that.

God helped me to provide for my mom, first and foremost, to get all kinds of costly, holistic herbs for her (paid out of my own pocket) in order to help avoid traveling to the doctor. So unless she is terribly sick, she doesn't want to go out for any doctor's visits, and I cannot blame her. I was overwhelmingly stressed out each time I had to give her a ride. It made me feel guilty no matter how perfectly I drove—despite minimal braking and the steadiest speed I could muster through daily traffic.

In accordance with motion sickness, she had not gone anywhere with me growing up, except one major move to a new house. When she had to move to Seoul from Mokpo, back in Korea, my grandmother had my mother put in a sleeping train. Although I was big already, I was also squeezed into her one-passenger bed. That was the easiest way for her to travel long distances.

My mom has never gone on one shopping trip with me here in America. I am not just talking about outlet stores or fancy malls, but I am even talking about local supermarkets or the Walmart near my house. These could be the reasons my mom lacks the basic "common sense" that everyone else seems to have.

For example, in the middle of talking, if I mentioned the store Walmart, it had to be explained. What

Walmart is — it is more than a supermarket; they sell from A to Z at the lowest prices. The store is huge, demanding quite a walk and requiring a couple of hours for shopping sometimes. It's a popular store with locations everywhere. It's something that many people generally know about, even if they have never been there or shopped there, but she has no idea.

By extension, this also applies to knowledge or awareness of cultural how-tos or the norms of where we live. Having such low exposure to the way people act or live outside of our house, she is always confused about simple concepts. Each little thing we have to explain in detail, and we often end up arguing about something that she doesn't quite understand, like typical human behaviors. A small, silly example is how many people across the country eat pizza as a meal. For years, we would order pizza, and she'd ask, "Where's the rice?" To which we'd reply: "This is our rice." We laugh about it to this day.

There was this one time we went out for a family dinner: we went out together when my mom first came, but she threw up on the way, within five minutes. That became the first and last time. She didn't want to go out in the first place since she eats very little at a time; take-out or delivery is much, much easier for her. Sometimes, especially when it was her birthday, we went to a local restaurant together, within walking distance. It was a struggle for our family to have such limited options, but we tried our best. She says she doesn't care, but I still feel uncomfortable and guilty just leaving her at home whenever the rest of the family goes out to eat at various places, including relatives' houses we *all* are invited to.

People have asked me how she came to America: it's a miracle that happened by the grace of God. She had taken a special medication, putting extra patches all over her body, and had special acupuncture before getting on the airplane. I have never been able to go shopping, to nice restaurants (only a couple that were within walking distance from home), or to a movie with Mom, let alone travel with her (only once to the beach, as mentioned below), for my entire life. These activities are all a luxury to my poor mom. These are things that many families, parents, and children can enjoy together, but I feel like I missed out.

There is hardly any fun living with my mom. There is nothing much I can do for her at home except being an entertainer to help keep her occupied, 365 days a year, as a good daughter, and that's my challenge. Nevertheless, is this possible? *Ahh! God, what can I do? Help me, God!*

Give thanks to the LORD, for he is good. His love endures forever.

Psalm 136:1

May 2007: My Special Suggestion

It has been eight years since Mom came to live with me. Undoubtedly, she has been a great help with the children while I worked: they didn't have to go to a babysitter! But these days, I find myself wishing to have a break from her. My baby, Ashley, started middle school this year, and she is a very independent child. Richard *could* be more responsible if his grandmother didn't intervene so often on his behalf.

My mom has never left my home, even for one day, since she came. I love my mom, but I no longer miss her. This numb feeling toward her is sad and frustrating. Everybody needs a break from each other. That probably helps us to miss and love each other more.

Although my children go to school and my day off falls on Monday, a weekday, I can never be home alone because of my mom. I can never occupy any part of my home all by myself.

I can't help but be stressed that I have to be aware of somebody else in the same space all the time, even though it's my mom. There is no freedom for me, whether I stay home or go out, because Mom wants to know everything about me: where I'm going, why I have to go, and when I'll be back. If I am late, she asks why was I late and why couldn't I call her.

I never knew how hard it could be to live with my mom as a grown-up. She seemed to control me like her child, but I am *her* caregiver, taking care of her like my patient and child. Every. Single. Day.

After much thought, I carefully suggested a vacation to Mom for a couple of months to see her sisters and brother in Korea, and I offered to pay for everything. It is I who supports her fully, and there is no one to help me. *Despite the cost, I will get my respite from her so that I may carry on. I have to be wealthy just to care for my mom!*

With some doubt, I asked her the impossible, but her answer came before I even finished: "*No.*" She didn't care to go at all, even if I paid for it. Mom has absolutely no idea what I think or how my marriage suffers. Indeed it is better for her not to know it.

It must be true that she never misses her family because she doesn't miss her past — just like me. I knew it. It is hopeless. I wonder if anybody out there misses her. It's no use to think of it. Everyone is fully occupied with themselves.

Ironically, the situation is completely opposite on my mother-in-law's side. She and her siblings are very close, and each takes care of one another. Obviously, it is really interesting for me to observe two different life stories and see the contrasts. Sometimes I wonder about the experiences God is giving me and about the benefits of those experiences. *Oh God, what shall I do? Help me!*

Suddenly, I remembered my pledge for Mom and started to understand why God made me pledge for her.

> *Give thanks to the LORD, for he is good. His love endures forever.*
>
> **Psalm 136:1**

August 2007: A Vacation with Mom

After I had researched many potential vacations for my mom and family, including a cruise that I desperately wanted (I know, I was out of my mind), I finally planned a special vacation, our *first* vacation. Since my mom is so withdrawn and completely passive, I had to force her this time — the first time — to go with us to the beach for nine days. Otherwise, she would have never gone.

Richard, Ashley, and I — not my husband this time (he went for a golf trip instead) — were very excited to enjoy a long beach vacation. At this time, Richard was in high school, and Ashley was in middle school. This extra-lengthy vacation was possible because I rented one floor of a house: two bedrooms, a kitchen, a bathroom, and a living room, from my client who owns the house in Long Beach Island, New Jersey. I had never rented a beach house before. It was exciting!

Though I knew it was nearly a two-hour drive one way, I wanted to take a chance. I wanted to create a nice vacation to remember with Mom. If not, I would certainly regret it. There is no fun without effort, and there are no memories to share if you don't make them. Thus, I was determined.

Needless to say, it was a major trip for my mom with all her anti-motion sickness medicine, patches, and spray, which were a little more than she was used to. For the most part, we had prepared for the trip with much prayer. Therefore, when Mom did not get sick at all in my car getting there, I thought our prayers were answered! Truly, it was a miracle!

The house we stayed at was three blocks away from the beach. My mom said it was the first time she saw the ocean in her life.

The weather that week was unfortunate. It rained most of our stay, which resulted in outings to local shops and restaurants. Thank God my children brought their gaming systems: they didn't care whether they went to the beach or not. However, they still wanted to check out the entertainment in town, and I did not want to spend our time sitting around the house or cooking. So, out we went. The three of us. Traveling and dining out do not appeal to my mom, so she did not go anywhere with us. Consequently, for her, our vacation mimicked time spent at home.

During this vacation, I had to go back and forth to my salon business for half the time; although, I wish I didn't have to. When the weather finally became clear and sunny, walking for three long blocks to the beach was demanding for Mom because the sun was scorchingly strong, except during early morning or late evening. But my mom was neither a morning person nor an outdoorsy person.

If we made the trip back home safely, it would still have been perfect. On the contrary, going back home was too torturous for her. She got extremely sick, throwing up about three times, nearly dying in my car. She asked, "Are we home yet?" nearly a hundred times. I felt so guilty about my poor mom despite praying desperately. When she came home, she said, like a declaration, "I will *never* go anywhere ever again. Never ask me again."

That is why I became more stressed and depressed as a result of this trip. I really have no clue how to make my mom happy except being silly and clowning around at home.

August 2008: My Depression

I have never been so depressed like this. My life is too demanding, and I am overloaded more than I can bear by both home and business. Since my husband is the primary breadwinner and he is a faithful provider, he thinks my business is nothing more than a hobby. My business has been suffering financially, only offering a host of problems, so I can't mention it at home. My home only welcomes me with loads of housework every night, regardless of my physical or mental capacity. Simply put, nobody cares about me. Nobody asks me how I am. Rather than wanting to know me, everyone expects me to handle all of life's problems. They know only one word: "Me, me!" and demand endlessly. I'm not a human here.

Admittedly, the biggest problem of my life is my marriage. It tears me apart while I still want to make it work. No matter what I do, it seems hopeless. My husband and I don't fight as much as in the first decade of marriage, less than half the amount, and with time it grows less and less. But this second decade is still challenging now because of his indifference. I wonder if he can see me. He seems like a wall, a stone, a valley, an ocean, and mountains to me. He says he's stressed, and that's all he says as if he's the only one entitled to be stressed in this whole world. With that one word, he separates himself from me; then, he confines himself to his own cell.

For years I asked him to pray with me, but there was no use. He never seemed to be happy at the positive changes I fostered in my marriage and spiritual life. Instead of becoming happy at my improvements, he grew further away from me like a rebellious child. That's why we continuously go around in circles. I also assume he might be going through his own depression. So, in conclusion, he could never help me in any way, which begs reflection: *how can I help him while I'm also devastatingly needy?*

Oh, Lord! What shall I do? I'm hopeless. I don't want to live anymore. Take me. I want to go now. I don't want to come home.

As I sailed out for a cruise vacation (it was only my children and I), I didn't want to come back. I felt sorry for my children. *Lord, if you want, take us! Sorry, Mom!* I wasn't afraid of the Atlantic Ocean.

But the ship brought me back. Maybe it was the Lord. *Why, Lord!*

I came back more depressed from the trip and couldn't believe I had to continue what I had been doing all over again. One week of vacation didn't do anything to add or subtract from my life. Moreover, my depression became even worse.

Hurt from My Mom

What my mom told me today was so shocking. After I told her of my depression, she hurt me beyond measure. I couldn't tell her the details, just the facts. I suffered from severe depression accompanied by incessant crying. I wanted to be understood, and I needed any support I could get from her, my mom.

Instead of offering comfort or encouragement, she confronted me, saying she is sacrificing herself for everybody here with all the chores. She kept saying that she is not demanding nor bothering and that she lives as quiet as dead so that no one needs to worry about her. And, of course, she goes back to her mountain of self-pity. That's right. She is always the victim.

Really? Was that what she was thinking? How can somebody think exactly the opposite of somebody else? Does she have any idea about what I'm going through? Does she have any pity on me? How can she say that? What does she know about life? Does she know what responsibility is? Doesn't she know how she's provided for? Was she calculating all the labor that she was offering to me? Child care and house care? What was my mom thinking, truly? So she's sacrificing more than me? After everything I had done for her, is this what I get from her? She was so righteous. She's so selfish. I hate that she victimizes herself. She's the victim, as always. That's her sickness.

I'm so hurt. I can't do this anymore. I can't. God, help me! In the middle of it, quietly and gently, God made me remember the pledge.

Give thanks to the LORD**, for he is good; his love endures forever.**
1 Chronicles 16:34

Because of the LORD**'s great love we are not consumed, for his compassions never fail. They are new every morning; great is your faithfulness.**

Lamentations 3:22–23

September 25, 2008: My First Time Fasting and Grace

This is the memorable date that I received the special gift through the Holy Spirit after my very first partial fasting of ten days. It was the outpouring of the taste of heaven for a few days which swept away all my shortcomings at once. I could reconcile with my husband immediately and with ease. During my prayer that evening, the Holy Spirit showed me my unknown sins of the past like panoramas. The Holy Spirit made me acknowledge them so that my slate would be wiped clean. It was the most amazing thing that had happened to me yet. God rescued me timely from my trouble, depression! He never leaves nor forsakes me (Deuteronomy 31:6)! I experienced the power of fasting, which overcomes sin and fleshly desire, lifts the spirit, and follows the will of God.

The truth about the spiritual experience is that it doesn't last forever because, despite being spiritual beings, we also live in a fleshy world with fleshy problems. So the connection and the elation grow weak and weaker and are gone. Then, we long for a new, fresh, spiritual experience, a personal revival. That's life.

I have been crucified with Christ and I no longer live, but Christ lives in me. The life I now live in the body, I live by faith in the Son of God, who loved me and gave himself for me.
Galatians 2:20

Now faith is confidence in what we hope for and assurance about what we do not see.
Hebrews 11:1

And without faith it is impossible to please God, because anyone who comes to him must believe that he exists and that he rewards those who earnestly seek him.
Hebrews 11:6

January 2012: No More Business–A New Chapter

My last decade of marriage was in turmoil. I faced obstacles concerning my business, my mom, and my young children. God reached into the eye of the hurricane of my life and carried me out. He blessed me and my family through the storm. Life has been heavy and disorderly, but those times have passed; thank God! Everything is passing in God's realm. *How God is so faithful!* Finally, God led me out of my business of eight years which had become a long, dark tunnel. For this reason, the new year started very differently and so peacefully. Hallelujah!

My business was like an endless discipline course in submitting to God due to all the problems I encountered. It was the practice of yielding, deserting, and giving up on myself. Each time I faced a problem, I also had to face fear and my pride. Then, rather than being obedient to God at once, my flesh wished to do exactly the opposite of submission. Always arriving at the end of the cliff, I knelt down and surrendered. However, the result was unbelievable. The Holy Spirit must have helped me each time too. In contrast to the pain of obedience, God's promising reward was impossible peace and joy that surpassed all the turbulence and tribulations that had oppressed me.

That was why I was able to contain my complaints and wishes about my mom in the presence of my husband. God keeps changing me; *although, I asked Him to change my husband!* This household and my marriage are not boring but rather intriguing beyond my understanding. I wonder how this life has become functional, even peaceful. It's only God. I just thank God for that.

He surely granted me a brand-new chapter in my life. Hallelujah! Out of the blue, He made me join the nursing home ministry at church. This calling came on the first Saturday of this year when I visited the church for something else. Somebody asked me if I could come, and I answered that I could, as long as I was not busy. Of course, God canceled all my other appointments.

Years ago, without experience, I visited a different nursing home with the desire of helping elders, but it was too depressing to continue. I went with the expectation of developing a certain relationship with the patients. My experience didn't match my expectations.

I approached this new endeavor with no expectations, and it gave me pure joy! The elders there possess a special talent for humbling me and making me acknowledge that my mom and I are truly blessed. This ministry is definitely helping me to be grateful for my mom, as she stays in better condition than some of the elders there, and the gratitude I feel is a blessing in itself. *Thank You, Father!*

For we live by faith, not by sight.
2 Corinthians 5:7

Praise the LORD. Give thanks to the Lord, for he is good; his love endures forever.
Psalm 106:1

2013: My Wish

My mom has been extra difficult. I can hardly bear her these days. I keep wrestling against my flesh concerning her, day by day, with no more patience. My long-suffering over Mom has worn me out. She is testing me every day. *Does she have senses? Do I have to explain everything every time? The exact same thing, over and over, like explaining to a child? How much more, how frequently?*

There are many moments I just want to scream or yell at her. Surprisingly, in the midst of my stress, Grandmother appeared in my head — which was a shock in itself. *Was* she *frustrated at Mom like this?* It was the most awkward feeling that I could understand how Grandmother must have felt about my mom for the first time. Without God, without the Holy Spirit, the enemy drove, and she was out of control; she depended only on alcohol. She depended on the wrong thing.

Sometimes I desperately want my mom to go away from me, to leave my house, to go somewhere else, to visit a friend or a relative like everyone else does. My grandmother did that — left home once in a while. I suppose it was a relief for her; I know it was for me. However, I have to be occupied by my mother's presence 24/7, 365 days a year, for years, and it is like raising a baby who never grows old. Nobody can sustain a job like this. That's all I want, a temporary vacation from her. *Is it wrong?*

I have wished *that* numerous times. If I could have her for only half a year for the rest of my life, then it would be great. If somebody took her for a couple of months of the year, it would still be great. Only a month would be great too. I wish I had a sibling to share this burden of caregiving, but I am an only child. This is beyond what an ordinary daughter can bear. Nevertheless, I never think to abandon her, ever. God knows. I would rather keep her in my life forever. God knows. *Father, help me! Recharge me!*

> **Give thanks to the Lord, for he is good. His love endures forever.**
> **Psalm 136:1**

> **For we live by faith, not by sight.**
> **2 Corinthians 5:7**

2014: Leave Me Alone

It seems like she is in my way, in my small house, at all times. Whenever I stay home and am anywhere other than in my room, she's there. We often get to be in that awkward position of not knowing which direction to move to avoid a collision, especially in my tiny kitchen. My mom chooses to be there whenever I have to be in there even though she does not cook. It is just her favorite place. My mom knows no boundaries.

Why does she still want to be right next to me even though she lives with me and sees me every day? Really? What about me? I'm not her baby. I'm a grownup wanting to run away from her. Leave me alone! Please!

So she gets to stay and watch me whenever I am in the kitchen. We get to eat all three meals together on days when I am given the opportunity to stay home. Sometimes I just want to be by myself, enjoying my quiet time, not being bothered, not being conscious of somebody's presence. I guess I have no life nor freedoms.

I'm limited to living only a "daughter's life." Mom is the only one demanding of me these days — my husband goes away on business frequently, and both of my children are grown and preoccupied with their own lives. Their absence and lack of communication make me feel useless and sad. Yet, no matter how much I respect their privacy, *I* have no privacy of my own because of my mom.

If not for God, I really couldn't do this anymore because I know I'm not that good, falling short all the time. However, even at this moment of complaining, God is with me, that I know! And He knows everything about me, even things I don't want Him to know. I could never conceal the things in my heart nor hide my body from Him! *Then I should be better!*

I'm not a child spiritually anymore. I have progressed through the pre-teen stage and would venture to say that I am now a teenager! My thoughts and actions should reflect my spiritual maturation. I should be better than before.

Oh God, how can a person live without having some alone time, free time? So God, what can I do? I'm sorry. Mercy me!

Thank God, He still loves me even at this stage of my life, and He loves my husband just as much as He loves me. Surely He loves my mom and my children. And, of course, He loves my angry neighbor on the right side as much as the angelic neighbor to my left. Oh oh, He makes me shake my head every day!

I turn on my praise music loud enough to rock the house, remove stress, and lift me high and free. I dance and worship Him in freestyle! Whether my mom watches me or not!

Oh, Lord, I praise You! I am so free in You. Thank You, Father! I just want to rest myself under Your feathery wing! Thank You. Thank You for everything that I can enjoy! You are so faithful! I praise You! I'll go not by sight but by faith (2 Corinthians 5:7)!

I can do all this through him who gives me strength.

Philippians 4:13

Give thanks to the LORD, for he is good. His love endures forever.

Psalm 136:1

Let everything that has breath praise the LORD. Praise the LORD.

Psalm 150:6

2015: No More Chatting

After all this, I made a major decision to discontinue provision of my dutiful, life-long entertainment, which was chatting with Mom. I know it sounds odd that I describe chatting with my own mother as a duty or entertainment. And why *would* I want to purposely reduce communication? As I have previously stated, I worried tremendously about my mom as a child. As soon as she came to my home in America, I resumed how I had entertained her back home so many years ago. Now, our daily chatting was mostly for the purpose of comforting her and easing her loneliness and weakness. The amount of time I poured into my mom every day was equal to the efforts I had given as a child. However, I wondered how much real, valuable conversation we took away from it all. Was my time and conversation with her meaningful? Either way, my accumulated stress outweighed the benefits.

As I prayed for this matter, God showed me that I must refuse to gossip. I realized I was inadvertently sinning while talking with Mom because she often drove me to her past, and then we settled there, bitterly ruminating over Grandmother and what we had gone through. She keeps going back, simmering her story like a stew. Oh my goodness, it is a never-ending story of lament, torment, and bitterness. It ached my heart. So I pray earnestly for Mom that the Holy Spirit empowers her so that she can break free from all the chains in her way; He blessed me to be free from all.

My sensitivity to the Holy Spirit has confirmed that the Holy Spirit grieves over our meaningless talk and gossip since it does not prevail His plans for us. Thus, I became resistant to our chats from the depths of my heart. Additionally, my stress is making me desperate; I am running short of energy. Talking for hours with Mom every day is wearing me out, so my time runs short for everyone else. I'm growing so unhappy because of this.

Putting my new decision into practice has been challenging because my mom still has needs. *I must provide something to occupy her!* When I shared my decision with Mom that I would reduce my usual talking with her to less than half and not allow myself to gossip, she looked a little concerned. I felt sorry for her and knew this would be very hard on both of us. *Oh, God, help me not sin! Help me not feel so guilty for her!*

I started to leave her in the house more often than before—mostly to the privacy of my room—or ask her to leave *me* alone for a while. I had to because unless I vocalize it, she never knows my needs. *Oh God, give me wisdom not to sin. Help me to help Mom. Please provide everything or the person she needs! Please send a friend for her!*

Help me love my mom more. Help me live right! Help me live not by sight but by faith (2 Corinthians 5:7)!

Let Your will be done (Matthew 26:39).

Give thanks to the LORD, for he is good. His love endures forever.

Psalm 136:1

2016: No Space and No Boundaries

My mom doesn't seem to enjoy staying home as a shut-in, even though she has been living like that for all her life. Mentally, she challenges us to think of her just like a child. She waits for us eagerly, every day, as though it were something novel. Since she is entitled to be home alone all the time, she thoroughly misses each family member. It's because she has no job, no friends, and no acquaintances in her life. If she wanted a pet, I would provide her with one, but she is not an animal person. She is a plant person, minus the green thumb. Though she is an expert tailor, since she has come to America, she hasn't wanted to sew due to chronic fatigue from her handicap. Consequently, she occupies my time way more than I can bear. I have no choice but to be her "everybody."

If I go out, I must call her once every three or four hours. If I forget, I receive a voicemail in her most serious tone: "What happened to you? How come you didn't call me? Call me as soon as you can." These messages suck me out like a vacuum to where I feel no strength remaining in my body. She also keeps asking me to check on everyone else's busy schedule, day and

MY MOM & I

night, which I don't have to keep up with anymore: "When does Richard come home? When does Ashley come home?" No matter what we try, only my children and I are her business, especially me. So she gets into all of our business, whether we like it or not, as if she is our CEO or consultant. *Do I have to continue this reporting duty to her every day? At this stage of my life, do I have to tell Mom everywhere I go, every time? Can she care less about us? Really, I can't do this anymore!*

Surprisingly, I remembered my grandmother again. She must have felt exactly like me. At first, I wanted to shake her from my mind, but I couldn't because I felt something irresistible about her. I couldn't believe I felt compassion for her. She wasn't saved. She didn't know she needed a Savior, so she didn't have her personal Savior to cry out to. She didn't know that the Holy Spirit was available whenever she asked God to help her. How can a person overcome affliction in life without divine help while the enemy keeps attacking his or her vulnerabilities? How can a person overcome the control of the trap and plot of darkness; how can they overcome spiritual warfare without Him? They cannot (2 Corinthians 10:3–5).

Although more than a few times I have lectured my mom about everybody's space, needs, and boundaries, she doesn't seem to respond. Maybe she thinks that's not for a family. I gave up on it because I just hate that I have to repeat the same thing and have no energy to explain it over and over. It's a good thing my children started to step up, in my place, to tell Grandmother because they feel they have to. They give me my break. Thank God my children understand me. But my mom doesn't seem to appreciate it at all. Every time they explain things and give her admonishment, she takes it as nagging.

We live not by sight but by faith (2 Corinthians 5:7), I remind myself.

> **Give thanks to the Lord, for he is good. His love endures forever.**
> **Psalm 136:1**

2017: Goodbye Guilt

The enemy has been strong through Mom, pressing me with guilt and condemnation, even though I know that there is no condemnation in Christ Jesus.

When something bothers you over and over, and it torments you continuously, you become lost at some point. Even though you have been victorious in a thousand other ways, you become completely vulnerable to a thing *or person*. Especially when that beloved person challenges and disappoints you in the one area where you have asked for change millions of times. That's a fatal weakness like Achilles' heel. This scenario is familiar to me. It describes my reaction to my mom's self-pity. She can't empathize with anyone other than herself and her circumstances. And I internalize that to mean that I failed to make her happy. Whenever I faced her self-pity, it attacked me, and I lost myself to anger. Then it made me feel miserable and guilty again for wanting to give up on everything.

However, my conclusion is this. If our torment marks the end of it, then that is the result of choosing not to believe God anymore. There are only promises of God and the hope in Him in the life of believers who *keep* pursuing the faith by choosing to believe in Him (Hebrews 6:13-14, 18-19).

I couldn't hold this inside anymore, so I asked my small group to pray for me. I submitted my problem: no matter what I do for my mom, I feel guilty. I have this voice of condemnation telling me *I'm not good enough. You never make Mom happy.* I just can't escape this guilty feeling — that I was supposed to make her happy.

Then everyone prayed for me, all together! It was a powerful group prayer: "Our God is not the spirit of timidity, guilt, or condemnation! His Spirit is love, power, and a sound mind (2 Timothy 1:7)! Praise God! Amen! We trust You!"

Immediately the spirit of guilt, which is the devil, left me. From that moment, I had no more guilt. *Halle-lujah! Thank You, God! Thank You, my Father! We live not by sight but by faith (2 Corinthians 5:7)!*

Give thanks to the LORD, for he is good. His love endures forever.

Psalm 136:1

Therefore, there is now no condemnation for those who are in Christ Jesus.

Romans 8:1

"For my thoughts are not your thoughts, neither are your ways my ways," declares the LORD.

Isaiah 55:8

2018: His Love Endures Forever

Mom keeps asking me when she can live without oxygen tubes. *Didn't I explain it enough? Did she forget that it is the grace of God that extended her life with them and enhanced her health? How many times do I have to explain all these things?*

However, she embarrassed me, forcing me to ask the doctor again when we visited him last time as if she didn't believe me. She doesn't understand that she is aging with weak lungs. I am at a loss for words.

Mom, you know you're not aging backward! When will I hear her say she's grateful! Oh, God, forgive me! Give me more patience!

Give thanks to the LORD, for he is good. His love endures forever.

2018: A Big Praise Report

God has granted a miracle through the oxygen for my mom! Since summer, Mom has been sick with serious pneumonia. She started an extra new life with oxygen and tubes. It is inconvenient, but that was the way God granted a miracle and enhanced Mom's health overall.

Mom has a big oxygen machine for use at home and a portable mini machine for use on the road. She doesn't get motion sickness these days since she wears the oxygen tubes on her nose carrying the portable mini machine on the trip! That was a surprise and a miracle that we had prayed for her life! The oxygen supplied to her lungs seems to help her body function and prohibit an upset stomach too. Although she doesn't desire to travel far or long, it is still a blessing to be able to travel to her doctor without vomiting. *Hallelujah!* At last, I am free from the stress of driving her around! We can sing, praise, and pray joyfully on the run! What a tremendous difference! *Thank You, God, for this awesome present for Mom! You are faithful!*

It is another miracle that Mom can use a smartphone and watch YouTube at her age of nearly eighty! I never imagined that she could do this because she can't operate a computer. She doesn't even know how to turn one on or off. In addition, she used to hate watching TV, so I never thought she would be interested in either of these technologies.

It was Richard's idea and his effort—helping Grandma whenever she calls him instead of me. Definitely, my son is more patient with Mom (in certain areas) than I am.

Now, Mom loses herself in watching various Korean videos, including lots of teachings from Korean Christian programs all day long. We hear her laughter much more often. The happy virus is invading here!

Thank You, God! Praise God! We live not by sight but by faith (2 Corinthians 5:7)!

Give thanks to the LORD, for he is good. His love endures forever.
Psalm 136:1

I consider that our present sufferings are not worth comparing with the glory that will be revealed in us.
Romans 8:18

For it is by grace you have been saved, through faith—and this is not from yourselves, it is the gift of God.
Ephesians 2:8

5. God-Given Discernment (2018)

I was driving down the road. It was sunny, mid-day, and there was no traffic. I was listening to praise music and praying with questions to God, too, all at once. *Why is my life so hard, God? Is anybody's life harder than this?*

Instantly, a picture popped into my head. It was an obscure picture of a random child who was severely disabled both physically and mentally. I was frowning my forehead to see the face of the child more closely, but it was unclear and difficult to recognize.

Oh, how hard can it be? Immediately imagining the pain and agony of that person and family, I was hum-bled swiftly. Now, I was thinking something different. *How can they deal with a family member having a disability like that? How do they do it?*

As I asked, I perceived the answer at the same time; they do not expect anything from the family mem-ber who is impaired. The fact is a fact that cannot be changed. That person has to receive, and the others are to give, and they just live with the fact.

As soon as I finished the thought, the face of the child in the picture zoomed up to a clearer focus, and, sud-denly, there was my mom as a young girl. I was startled. I had never thought of my mom as a young girl but as an aged, handicapped person. But God revealed to me, so suddenly, her mentality that had been captured at the age of eleven when her fatal illness began. Her traumatic illness, paralysis, and the life-long abuse from my grandmother had bounded her. Furthermore, the endless, unique life-setting as a shut-in has never allowed her to grow freely. Until then, I had never imagined or acknowledged my mom's true status.

All at once, this discernment God gave me brightened my eyes with illuminating sparkles. *She has never passed adolescence.* This suddenly explained her behavior all this time. My children had asked my mom numerous times, jokingly: "Grandma, how old are you? How could you do that? Are you five years old?" It had been their joke, but *my* endless frustration—the missing information about Mom's hidden captivity that only God knew. Without perceiving who my mom is and how my mom is, I have felt challenged endlessly. Foolishly, I have lived in frustration believing her potential because of my fantasy. It was my selfishness and greediness to demand something she couldn't offer. After all, I could find *my* problem. It was my disappointment. It was due to an expectation of my mom that satisfied my wish for her to be the "ideal mom." I allowed myself to be disappointed, and that was how I allowed the foothold of the enemy to press me (Ephesians 4:27).

My expectations were built upon my fantasy about my mom, which had been formed by my misconceptions when I was young. I had seen all my aunts—Mom's younger sisters, my mom is the oldest of eight—coming to my mom for counseling. At least four of them, in turn, had kept coming to her, pouring out their problems. Back then, I had no idea they were throwing their own pity parties in front of Mom. My mom had just been their safety net, a safe space to vent. However, in my child-like view, my mom had seemed to counsel them well. Since my mom had been the only one going to church consistently among them, praying religiously to Mary, with no resistance to Grandmother's abuse, she had looked like a real saint to me. I had thought my mom must be so wise to be a counselor for them, and I was so proud of her.

Though I learned that I could not expect anybody other than God to satisfy me, I failed to apply it to my relationship with my mom. I have surrendered my family members to God, one by one, during the course of my life, but not Mom. Rather, I have burdened her with more responsibility than anybody. Without surrendering Mom to God, I hurt myself with foolish disappointment, and that disappointment was a barrier to compassion. So that was the foothold I put out to the enemy, which has made me focus on the ugliest side of Mom and kept me in a constant state of stress. My heart broke in humility for my mom. I sobbed for the child within my mom. She is purely innocent. *I'm so sorry, Mom. Forgive me. You are still my mom, and now you are understood more than ever before. I free you, and I love you so much more!*

I'm sorry, my Father, my God! Forgive me! Forgive my selfishness and my disappointment, Father! I'm not respon-

sible for Mom; You are! I surrender Mom to You. He is so gracious. He understood me and my weakness and said: "That's my child, my daughter!" As I repent it, He no longer remembers it; He removes it so far away. He doesn't love me more than my worst day or less than my best day. His love is not changing! His love is never failing! He has never stopped loving me nor my mom! I praise God for His non-stop love! Hallelujah!

Although God revealed my mom's shortcomings, she has a very clear memory and reasonable comprehension and opinions as it relates to her and her family's past history. This has caused endless confusion for me in understanding her because it didn't match her comprehension in different areas of life. Therefore, I must confirm and verify my mom's memory and her concern as accurate in regard to her family's past history and as a testimony to her prior experiences.

> *For I know my transgressions, and my sin is always before me.*
>
> **Psalm 51:3**

> *Cleanse me with hyssop, and I will be clean; wash me, and I will be whiter than snow.*
>
> **Psalm 51:7**

> *The LORD is compassionate and gracious, slow*

to anger, abounding in love.

Psalm 103:8

For as high as the heavens are above the earth, so great is his love for those who fear him; as far as the east is from the west, so far has he removed our transgressions from us.

Psalm 103:11–12

How much better to get wisdom than gold, to get insight rather than silver!

Proverbs 16:16

"Though the mountains be shaken and the hills be removed, yet my unfailing love for you will not be shaken nor my covenant of peace be removed," says the LORD, who has compassion on you.

Isaiah 54:10

My command is this: Love each other as I have loved you. Greater love has no one than this: to lay down one's life for one's friends. You are my friends if you do what I command.

John 15:12–14

"In your anger do not sin": Do not let the sun go down while you are still angry, and do not give the devil a foothold.

Ephesians 4:26–27

Submit yourselves, then, to God. Resist the devil, and he will flee from you.

James 4:7

6. God's Perfect Plan for My Mom and Me

For the Beginning

Every once in a while, when I thought about Mom's life, it reminded me of the sad truth: that she has no place to go and has nobody other than me to take care of her. Thank God she has me! *Only God knows!* However, she has six sisters and two brothers in Korea. As far as I know, except maybe for one, nobody seems to know God yet because they don't even let me talk about Him. This is heartbreaking to me, but they have no idea.

But God must have plans for them. If they knew God loves each and every one of them unconditionally, as equally as me and my mom, they wouldn't be able to resist Him. They need to know that God doesn't love Mom and me more than God loves them. I know that God's heart must be aching crazily for each missing child right now! It is written in the Bible as the word of God (Matthew 18:12).

Among my mom's household, nobody had ever known that there is only one God, nor did they know of His master plan. They never wanted to know Him because they didn't need Him. Although my grandmother and aunts had attended a Catholic church near their house for some time, it was only as a religious activity; they had never met Jesus personally as their Savior.

Thus, this was God's perfect plan for Mom and me.

Mom's illness was part of the plan. God had allowed my mom's misery. Enemies caused misery and unfortunate things, but God turned it into a good thing for Mom and me. If Mom was healthy like her other siblings, she would not have wanted God as much as she did. If Mom had not been so continuously desperate, she would not have needed God so much in her life. It had been the despair of her heart that God used to bring her out of the deep darkness of many generations so that she could hang out with Him. After God separated Mom from the household spiritually, He brought me forth to Mom, so she was able to raise me with the faith of the one and only God with His Son as my Savior, Jesus!

Oh God, my Father! I pray for my aunts, my uncles, and my cousins! Touch their hearts now and let them know You are near. Let them know You have never left nor forsaken them! Let them know each one of them is so loved by You. No matter how far they went, no matter how they hated You! Almighty God! Let them know Your love that sacrificed Your only Son who knew no sin to save them while they never wanted to know You! Let them know Your magnificent love that can wash off all their sin as You washed mine!

For the Present and the Future

I am astonished at God and His perfect plan for my mom and me: He even made me pledge to Him for my mom since His plan is perfect for her, but I'm not perfect!

I am sorry to God if I delayed Him and His plan with my selfishness and unwillingness from time to time.

But it is written: He knew everything, my inner thoughts, the very motives, and all the days of my life from the very beginning (Psalm 139). It has been God who has taken care of my mom and me and my family so faithfully through it all. I'm thankful to be well taken care of by my God, who has never left nor forsaken me, especially during the time of living with my mom. I have been reminded by Him, when needed, of the pledge I made to Him. Not because He chastises, but because He knew my course wasn't easy! So He has helped me faithfully. He has kept me in this race, whether piggyback style or with wings like eagles, so as to finish this race. He has also run alongside me, cheering me, just like an intimate Father ready to welcome and award me at the end of the race.

God also knew that He made us to love and take care of our children naturally — we get to know them better while raising them, which makes understanding them easier than understanding our parents. It is easier to send love downwards than upwards. That is why so many people feel challenged when it comes to caring for their elderly parents. Without the word of God, without looking at the cross, it would have been impossible to keep the place where I had to be: if anyone would come after me, he must deny himself and take up his cross daily and follow me (Luke 9:23). The love of God in me enabled me to follow Him and to maintain my ordained position as caregiver.

This daily spiritual warfare with my mom has been somewhat hard for me, but suddenly — suddenly is the way of God's working — the chapter of my life is recreated, dramatically, optimistically, and with discernment as His infinite wisdom provides answers to all of my questions. This is what God does! God's given discernment solves all puzzles! However, His given discernment is not a magic wand. His wisdom guides me to lower my expectations of Mom and yield to her each time we face difficulties.

Most of all, God has allowed all the problems in my life and has used them to draw me closer to Him and build me up to who I am today. Without those problems, I could not have built this strong faith that has enabled me to do everything (Philippians 4:13). What God enabled me to do well was this very basic but important ministry of my home and family, which I was selected for, and only I can do well. Now I sense a certain *future* ministry that He is going to assign me drawing nearer. I feel that what I'm writing is a part of it, so that excites me! Indeed, He worked out all things together for all my good (Romans 8:28)!

In the end, I have learned that it was *so* true: Jesus came to give us a life that we can live fully, happily, and abundantly (John 10:10). It took so long for me to find this simple truth! I discern more about the will of God! He wants and allows us to taste heaven while we live here today. It is surely possible as long as His word is in me and I am in Him (John 15:7). *Ahh, thank You, my God, my Father! Hallelujah, hallelujah!*

This is an addition written at the time of the coronavirus pandemic of 2020. There have been trials in my life that have demanded my obedience to the point of tears, and it has not been easy while I have longed for His promises. Upon this pandemic, I acknowledged suddenly that I am living out His plan for me. I know this because of the surpassing peace I feel, a peace that is beyond understanding, a peace that only His sovereignty can provide. Before, it had always been future tense for God's plan for me, but suddenly I felt His plan prevail over the present I was living in.

So I want to tell everyone, even though some are crying at this moment: hang on! You are not alone! Let me pray for you! We are going through this together because He is with us! We can, with His help! We will overcome it and see His faithfulness!

Humbly, I thank Mom for her choice of me. She had never not wanted me from conception, but she loved me enough to take a risk and to give birth in her condition. There is no one who has loved me more or who has sacrificed more for me than my mom. She was the very guide who led me to faith through Jesus Christ. Without my mom, I could never be who I can be today. Mom, you are the best mom for me! I don't want any other mom than you. I love you, Mom, more than ever, truly and eternally!

My husband — soon-to-be-saved — is a good and faithful man, but our personality differences create mountains between us. God has started to move those mountains. I'm ever more confident to live with him (and my children) forever to eternity because I'm now ever more mature in my faith and have the closest relationship with the Lord Jesus, my God!

"For I know the plans I have for you," declares the LORD, "plans to prosper you and not to harm you, plans to give you hope and a future."
Jeremiah 29:11

So he said to me, "This is the word of the LORD to Zerubbabel: 'Not by might nor by power, but by my Spirit,' says the LORD Almighty."
Zechariah 4:6

You hem me in behind and before, you lay your hand upon me.

Psalm 139:5

For you created my inmost being; you knit me together in my mother's womb. I praise you because I am fearfully and wonderfully made; your works are wonderful, I know that full well. My frame was not hidden from you when I was made in the secret place, when I was woven together in the depths of the earth. Your eyes saw my unformed body; all the days ordained for me were written in your book before one of them came to be. How precious to me are your thoughts, God! How vast is the sum of them!

Psalm 139:13–17

Not only so, but we also glory in our sufferings, because we know that suffering produces perseverance; perseverance, character; and character, hope. And hope does not put us to shame, because God's love has been poured out into our hearts through the Holy Spirit, who he has been given to us.

Romans 5:3–5

Accept one another, then, just as Christ accepted you, in order to bring praise to God.

Romans 15:7

[...] being confident of this, that he who began a good work in you will carry it on to completion until the day of Christ Jesus.

Philippians 1:6

Blessed is the one who perseveres under trial because, having stood the test, that person will receive the crown of life that the Lord has promised to those who love him.

James 1:12

Now there is in store for me the crown of righteousness, which the Lord, the righteous Judge, will award to me on that day—and not only to me, but also to all who have longed for his appearing.

2 Timothy 4:8

His Rod & Staff

I delight greatly in the LORD; my soul rejoices in my God. For he has clothed me with garments of salvation and arrayed me in a robe of his righteousness, as a bridegroom adorns his head like a priest, and as a bride adorns herself with her jewels.

Isaiah 61:10

For the message of the cross is foolishness to those who are perishing, but to us who are being saved it is the power of God.

1 Corinthians 1:18

For I am not ashamed of the gospel, because it is the power of God that brings salvation to everyone who believes: first to the Jew, then to the Gentile.

Romans 1:16

1. My Born-Again Experience (2000)

Part 1

Although I'd maintained my faith for decades, I was clueless about the true meaning of being born-again or of salvation. What I knew was that everyone's salvation or born-again experience was unique and different. However, I didn't fully grasp how simple, powerful or joyful it was until I had my own experience.

As I wrote in the beginning, I was born and raised Catholic at my grandmother's house in South Korea. A Catholic church in my hometown actually shared its rear fence as a mudstone wall at the end of my grandmother's house. Growing up, I attended this church until high school, until I left my hometown. The few times I skipped church can be counted on just my fingers.

Like a friendly next-door neighbor, my church was open for fellowship (caroling, Saturday school, youth groups, etc.) but served only as a temporary refuge. It hosted precious memories and then sent me home, where I was lonely, introverted, and pessimistic. I had never known about true joy — not even an ordinary joy from an ordinary life.

When my husband asked me to marry him, I asked him if he would go to the Catholic church with me, and he agreed gladly. He took some classes at Catholic church in order to marry me before the wedding. Then, we made an unanticipated choice to attend a Korean Presbyterian church when we came to the U.S. in 1989, where we lived in New York City for the first year.

We joined that church because we were invited by a pastor through a relative who picked us up at the airport. Until then, I had never thought of going to a Protestant church, but it was not easy to refuse that kind of persuasive offer. Furthermore, my husband said it would be temporary. Being directionally and vehicularly challenged, I gave up insisting on my idea. Before we knew it, we were newly christened — both of us.

When we moved to New Jersey a year later, our Korean pastor introduced us, yet again, to another Korean Presbyterian church near where we lived. I had doubted that my husband had any desire to go to a church in the first place, not having displayed any faith previously, but he seemed more eager than me at the beginning of our immigration to the United States.

There is some accuracy to the social myths that suggest people with an East Asian background will gather at ethnic churches in an effort to expand their social circle. I have met both men and women who have confirmed that this is the reason *they* started to come to church. Church-going was a way for them to meet others who shared their language, traditions, and interests. Without a support system like the church, these people felt lonely and disconnected from their home country and culture. My husband and I could certainly empathize with these feelings of isolation.

However, I had believed in my heavenly Father, my God, and everything He had done from the first time I had heard about Him as a very young child. When my mom told me that He was essentially my Father, Father-God, the sound lulled my young soul, the soul of a "fatherless" child. Consequently, I leaned on Him for my needs. To believe and love Jesus as the Son of God, my Savior who died on the cross for my sins and was resurrected, was easy for me as an innocent child. Every time I watched movies about Him, I sobbed terribly.

Even then, at the same time, I thought I was a good person. I thought: *I'm not so bad*. Hence it didn't change my personality or affect my life significantly, and I still didn't know about joy.

That had been why I was going to church — to perform my duty to God — and I felt good about it. That was the only thing I could boast about to anybody previously. I was proud to belong to my church. Going to church was normal to me. I was ticking boxes, but I never knew joy. If I missed church, I felt afraid and guilty immediately, as if I committed some kind of crime or received a bad grade.

It was the same thing with my husband. Sunday after Sunday, here in America, we dragged ourselves and our children to church dutifully, but we didn't even know why we were doing it. It was just a "church life," only to be acknowledged by the pastor and other church fellows, and we were even respected by them. Despite all the good parts, we were unhappy. We were simply afraid of God's punishment if we did not behave well, and we didn't want to miss out on God's blessings due to disobedience. Nevertheless, my family attended a Korean church for almost twelve straight years. We just kept on going to church. We were bound by the responsibility of my husband's position at the church, the children's education, and our relationship with some extended church family, but not by much else.

Out of all my church life, my most challenging word from the Bible was "joy" or "rejoice." Every time I heard or read about it, I felt irritated. "Rejoice in the Lord always!" (Philippians 4:4) and "Be joyful in hope!" (Romans 12:12) annoyed me. While I was growing up in turmoil and living in America as a poor young immigrant, the word "joy" was never mine. In fact, it mocked me and laughed in my face! The concept of joy sounded so unrealistic. One day, out of frustration, I had the courage to ask one of the pastors' wives if it was really possible to be joyful at all times, and I just told her my honest opinion that I think it is impossible and that the verse in the Bible must be a mistake or a joke.

My born-again experience occurred at the last Korean church I went to when I was visiting only for the third time. My husband suggested visiting that church once because his friend had invited him. But I made a huge fuss because there was somebody who I knew there who was very hard to get along with.

The young pastor's sermon was very different. Until then, most of the sermons I had heard were mostly about the blessings we would receive if we kept being faithful and serving well. However, this sermon was all about how much we sin and how desperately we need the blood of Jesus. Nevertheless, I thought, *Not me. I am not that bad! Who is he talking about?*

It was the beginning of the year 2000, and I was in my early thirties.

Not too long before that sermon, I had a distinct memory of my thoughts from months ago while in my previous church's parking lot. Even though they were only my thoughts while talking to God, they were stuck in my head, like a picture in my mind. It was as if somebody seized the instant for me.

As I was getting out of my car and walking into the church sanctuary, I paused to sigh deeply. I was fatigued and dragging myself along because it was such a duty to attend Sunday service after a long tiring week. Then, I looked up to the sky and talked to God in my mind. *Aren't I a good person, Father God? How can I be better? I can't be any better than this! I can't. I don't harm anybody. I help whoever You show me. Oh no, please, never expect me to be any better than this! I am doing my best!*

That moment was captured within me, and it played so vividly every time I remembered it—more precisely than a picture, but like a slow-motion video (which was very weird). Maybe I drew God's attention, or He became seriously concerned about me, though He didn't answer me at all.

This new sermon at the new church disturbed me. Even so, it touched and engrossed my soul. Irresistibly wondering what else the pastor would preach in the following weeks, I desired to visit the church once more.

Hence, I had to beg my husband to go there once more, only to find myself being tortured by another sermon. Surprisingly the pastor was preaching almost exactly the same thing again: we sin day and night, by the way we drink or eat a meal, by our actions, by our tongue, and by our thoughts. To God, hating somebody in our thoughts is the same as killing. Though we are saved once, every time we sin, and every type of sin necessitates the blood of Jesus. We should live a life of sanctification daily!

I could not believe that I was so bad, needing His cleansing blood, again and again.

I felt angry, thinking, *I'm different,* because, deep in my mind, there was somebody I could compare myself to, and that was my grandmother. How can my grandmother and I be equally the same sinners to God? It's impossible and so absurd to be compared to her. It was too humiliating to even think about her.

Out of deep frustration, I had to do something, thinking that I could prove myself. Out of the blue, an idea popped into my mind that made me laugh. Proudly, I wished to be examined (if there was a machine to test me, kind of like a lie detector), but it could be costly. Therefore, I decided to hire "me," myself, at no expense, as a self-investigator, to watch over myself every minute for a week. I would hold myself accountable! Being fascinated by that simple and convenient idea, I was delighted to think that I could prove myself. Thinking of my grandmother, I was confident that I was different and a better person.

During work that week, I was merrily caring for all my nail clients with the best patience. When a receptionist called me to answer the phone, it was my husband. As soon as I talked to him, he annoyed me very badly. He was going to be late again because of a company dinner! My frustration grew as, over time, he began to irritate me and hurt my feelings with numerous disappointments. I felt that he prioritized work over me and the children. He seemed not to care about our two young children or that I was a working mom. Being sociable is good, but he was so far off from the family-oriented person I expected him to be. After I hung up, I tried my best to cool down and get back to work.

Right at that moment, I was caught in a vision of myself raging in boiling anger. I witnessed myself murdering my husband in the heat of the moment. According to the sermon of that young pastor, I killed him with my anger, even if it was only in my mind. So shocked at looking at myself in the crime scene, I couldn't deny that it was me! It had been the very first time I watched myself being caught red-handed through the invisible video camera of me, both self-investigator and suspect.

Never having realized this all before, I was scared of myself. The offending party had always been my husband, who was acting selfish, with no consideration for me. He never knew what I liked or disliked. He just made me feel angry and upset.

Shaking my head and biting my lip, I was determined to be keener and more careful than before, so I would not be caught again. However, before the day was over, I was caught more than a few times because of some annoying and challenging clients. And by the end of the week, I was completely exhausted, being caught by me, myself, and my conscience, here and there, over and over.

Part 2

I found myself visiting the same church for the third week. If I didn't feel a burden to revisit the same church, I could simply refuse, but by mysterious means, I was driven to go there again. This time I sat in the same sanctuary with quite a different demeanor. It was only a week ago when I left so confident, but I came back as a very different version of myself.

I felt guilty. There was no doubt. I was completely guilty. Guilty me. It felt as if the pastor were speaking to me directly, convicting me! Bowing my head down, I closed my eyes. Suddenly, there in my mind, with closed eyes, I saw a wilderness. Then, I saw me drop, there in the middle of the wilderness. I looked terribly afraid, not knowing what to do, and started running away to escape the scene in my mind. I was looking for any place that I could hide myself from God in the vast wilderness, but it was pointless. It was so open and spacious with an endless horizon on all sides. I kept running, gasping with short breaths. I could not deny it, but I could not bear all the guilt that had been displayed in me. Imagining all of the accumulated sins of my life, I thought *I'd rather flee*. Running all this time had exhausted me, but no matter how fatigued I felt, I just couldn't stop.

Instantaneously, I saw myself in my mental picture arriving at the edge of a cliff. There was no other place to go. I was completely helpless and devastated. I had never been so desperate. I gave up on myself, falling on my knees. Then, I admitted it. *Yes, that's right. I am a sinner. I'm so bad.*

I could hardly breathe and sighed with sorrow to God, and then I thought, *What is next? What shall I do?*

I was trembling, not knowing what more to do beyond this point. I felt afraid. I had never been so afraid of God discovering my vast sinfulness.

Bowing my head down, I continued to close my eyes. Suddenly, I sensed a warm light had poured over me. It was so bright I wanted to close my eyes even tighter as if I had another set of eyes to close. I thought to myself, *Why is it so bright? Where is this light coming from?* As I was searching for the source of the light pouring out, still closing my eyes very tightly, all the way back, I peeked and saw the cross that poured out its shine and overwhelming brightness. It was the warmest and most beautiful, brilliant light! The light fell like a waterfall from the cross to bathe me and penetrate into all my bones and cells! I was saturated in the light.

Later I found the verses in the Scripture that match this experience:

If we confess our sins, he is faithful and just and will forgive us our sins and purify us from all unrighteousness.
1 John 1:9

For the word of God is alive and active. Sharper than any double-edged sword, it penetrates even to dividing soul and spirit, joints and marrow; it judges the thoughts and attitudes of the heart.
Hebrews 4:12

At that time, I still didn't process what had just

happened to me because I was waiting for some kind of punishment to follow my repentance and feeling of terrible guilt. So I was still thinking, *Is that all? Don't I need anything, God? You don't punish me? You're not mad at me? Are You sure? Is this it? Was it supposed to be this simple? I only said that I'm a sinner!*

I couldn't believe it. How gracious my Father-God can be!

At that moment, all at once, I felt I was changed. I was like a "before and after" picture in a magazine. I felt new! "The old has gone, the new has come in Christ Jesus" (2 Corinthians 5:17).

And then, so swiftly, I felt something rising within me. That was the energy, called joy, that I had never possessed. It affected me like hallucinogens of total happiness, surpassing all my limitations and expectations. It was coming from a well of joy in my heart. A well, which had been hidden and I had never known before, was pouring out uncontrollably. It was the joy I had never known in my life overflowing within me! *Wow! It's real! I feel overwhelming joy! The Bible was never wrong about joy. Hallelujah, I finally found true joy!*

Since the service wasn't over, I could hardly wait, wanting to jump out of my seat! When it was over, I was gamboling (not gambling!) and laughing with new joy like a wild lunatic. I absolutely could not hide how happy I was and wanted to tell everybody. However, my husband, who was sitting right next to me, still had no idea what had just happened to me and refused to believe me, covering his ears. I realized that joy had to be given by God. It is only God who can click on our hearts with His own remote when we repent, as a great reward!

Consequently, no matter who believed me, my spiritual life was changed immediately from that day onward. All I wanted was to worship and praise Him. I couldn't wait until another Sunday to worship Him. Now the time between Sunday to Sunday seemed too long, and I began to go to church during the week. Before, I was mostly late to service, as if being dragged there, and I couldn't wait for it to be over. But after that experience, I didn't want to miss anything because I enjoyed being in His presence, and it was now my privilege to worship Him. I had never known that worshipping my God could be the happiest thing for me. I thought that the new church would be my last church until I went to heaven.

But most sadly, after two years, that church congregation ended up splitting into two halves. Differing from my side of the group, the other half of the congregation hated the pastor and his sermons. The young pastor, whom I loved, resigned and left. That was why my family left that church also.

Worse yet, it affected my husband drastically — along with other accumulated undesirable things within the church — enough to make him end up quitting on church life itself. It was unfortunate for him to encounter several negative church experiences before he was saved. He said, "Enough is enough." He never received the same experience as me that day, and our viewpoints on church diverged.

Unexpectedly, the church life can hurt people since the church is a gathering of people. If a majority of the group is not born again yet or matured yet, it can cause disagreements and hurt feelings. As for me, from that day forward, nothing could stop me from worshiping God.

Part 3

I wanted to share my born-again experience with my daughter when she entered high school. After I prayed about how I should present it in the most effective way, God gave me these illustrations.

There are two different pictures of me: before I was born-again and after I was born-again.

The "before" me: I am standing right under the cross where Jesus is dying, and I am crying for Him on Calvary. He is suffering and dying for everybody, including me. There is a massive number of people surrounding me. I am in the "good group." Next to my group, there is a group "less good" than mine, then lesser and lesser. Far from me, at my opposing side, is the "worst group," and I don't even want to meet their eyes at all.

The "after" me: I am standing right under the cross where Jesus is dying for my sin. I am bowing my head down and crying for Him on Calvary. And slowly, I am trying to find some people who can back me up because I feel so ashamed. I look all around. But hopelessly, I find no one. There is only Jesus and me. And Jesus says, "It is all for you!" I finally realize that my sin alone made Him die on the cross!

The Bible says, "For the wages of sin is death [...]" (Romans 6:23). This means God is holy, and holiness is God. He does not sin. Our God and sin can not reside together. That's why we became separated from God following Adam and Eve. But God himself prepared the way for us to restore the relationship with Him. That's Jesus, who bore all our sins and died for us on the cross but is risen.

"[...] but the gift of God is eternal life in Christ Jesus our Lord" (Romans 6:23).

God has prepared the ultimate sacrifice for His sinful people. And the sacrifice was His own Son, Jesus, who knew no sin and was sinless (2 Corinthians 5:21). He left his place in heaven and took all the punishment along with contempt and insult as a human being. He paid the price completely until He dropped the last drop of His holy blood for our sins, for the perfect sacrifice for sinners like us! He rose on the third day and is living today.

How much did God love me, this wretched sinner,

to pay with His Son's blood? So that I could live! This unbelievable love of God is the "Amazing Grace."

Through this born-again experience, I was able to possess overflowing joy and was set free from all the shame. I began to walk the very first steps toward His Holiness.

John 3:16–18 says,

For God so loved the world that he gave his one and only Son, that whoever believes in him shall not perish but have eternal life. For God did not send his Son into the world to condemn the world, but to save the world through him. Whoever believes in him is not condemned, but whoever does not believe stands condemned already because they have not believed in the name of God's one and only Son.

But I trust in your unfailing love; my heart rejoices in your salvation.

Psalm 13:5

In him our hearts rejoice, for we trust in his holy name.

Psalm 33:21

So you too should be glad and rejoice with me.

Philippians 2:18

Rejoice in the Lord always. I will say it again: Rejoice!

Philippians 4:4

Rejoice always.

1 Thessalonians 5:16

Rejoice over her, you heavens! Rejoice, you people of God! Rejoice, apostles and prophets! For God has judged her with the judgment she imposed on you.

Revelation 18:20

2. My Very First Holy Spirit Encounter

I speak the truth in Christ—I am not lying, my conscience confirms it through the Holy Spirit.

Romans 9:1

After my biggest life event of being born-again in 2000, I was getting ever more frustrated at my marriage because I couldn't change anything by myself, even with my new awareness of living a holy life. My life became full of complexity due to a new business, growing children, and an additional household member (my mom started living with us). While we needed teamwork in our busy lifestyle, my husband and I were still clashing and not cooperating like intimate partners.

Our pain and hurt continued. The truth is that we still can get hurt by circumstance as long as we wear flesh, regardless of everlasting, God-given joy. Though my spiritual life had changed immediately to joy—this

189

kind of joy remains in you, never to vanish and can be restored at any time as God heals you — I could not instantly help my personal life with my husband.

I can laugh now to look back and tell this, but I have lots of empathy for the younger me and the younger him. We were merely twenty-one and twenty-five years old, very close to my children's ages now, though I still consider them my babies! Not only were we trying out a brand new life in a brand new country (as poor immigrants), but we also had no idea we had been thrown into tough spiritual warfare. It's not painful to talk about the story now, but it was excruciating then, at the beginning of our marriage.

"For our struggle is not against flesh and blood, but against the rulers, against the authorities, against the powers of this dark world and against the spiritual forces of evil in the heavenly realms" (Ephesians 6:12).

When we came to America as newlyweds, in 1989, everything changed rapidly in the panorama of our lives. It was supposed to be the happiest time for us, but realistically there was no time for my husband and me to relax or adjust to a new way of living in a new world. Working hard, as blue-collar workers, we couldn't see each other or spend quality time together. Then, before we knew it, our two children were born one by one, a little earlier than we originally planned.

In my twenties, I couldn't imagine what my husband had to go through because of my immature

"What about me?" attitude. Personally, I went through three kinds of shock at the beginning of life in America.

First, I was married, and marriage bore a significant responsibility. As a Korean wife, I had to take care of my husband, though I was a novice at homemaking. I had zero basic life skills. Furthermore, I wasn't interested in fulfilling this role I was expected to fill. Most Korean wives traditionally take care of everything for their husbands at home. The new trend was that the majority of men (of my generation) were changing to help their wives, but not my husband. He was raised a different way. He maintained the beliefs of the older generation, so his interests were far from home. This was my biggest complaint for decades; although, I didn't realize it at that time.

Second, I came to a new world, America, which made me feel incompetent and foolish. Later, all of the immigrants we met shared with us their experiences of feeling "dumb" in this new land.

Third, my mom wasn't here. She was still in Korea across the ocean. In addition, we didn't have a home phone for about six months while waiting for some processing. It felt like punishment to be unable to call my mom and friends. I couldn't ever imagine, throughout all of my life, not being able to call her. Some nights after a hard day's work, when I was by myself waiting for my husband until midnight or 1 a.m., all I did was cry.

Now, it is heartbreaking to recall how immature

we were. We truly had no idea about spiritual warfare, and it is scary to envision how vulnerable we were to the forces behind the scenes. That was why there was no way to handle the frustration and stress. It came from both sides, yet we could not recognize the source. It was not of this world. Being chased by frustration from the claustrophobic feelings of life, all we did was fight (when we found time after sixty-hour work weeks). To make matters worse, we were both hot-tempered, prideful, stubborn, and self-righteous, so we never knew how to yield to each other in a fight.

In my mind, my husband was becoming so different from the man I had dated, despite us having to rush to get married for the preparation of coming to America. In my memory, he had been very considerate and romantic, but everything proving him to be the opposite threw me into a stream of confusion.

As a minor example, when we shopped together, I still wanted to buy some inexpensive candles and flowers — only once in a while — even though there was not enough money for groceries. So we fought over it. All the Korean people I shared this with said that's characteristic of the traditional Korean man.

Thereafter, whenever my husband behaved or talked inconsiderately or unfairly to me, I became hurt and angry. Then, I would say something without thinking to make him angrier. We never knew when or how we started to fight or why we were fighting once we were caught up in the anger. In spite of never being physical, we would hurt each other brutally with screaming, yelling, and crying in boiling rage, regardless of where we were, while shopping, while in the car, while going to church, until someone we knew showed up and intervened.

As a result, our children became victims — especially Richard — of our mad foolishness. Ashley still remembers that we fought a lot when she was very young, but she said we fought less and less as time went on. On the other hand, Richard, almost five years older than Ashley, was devastated by his parents fighting for the first decade of his life. In the midst of our arguments, poor Richard would burst into horrible crying, and I would comfort him while antagonizing my husband simultaneously. Despite the fact that my heart was breaking for my son, I could never bring myself to yield to my husband, all the while thinking *I'm not wrong*.

As soon as I cooled down after the fighting, I was more crushed than ever. It was then that I could understand my actions from a different point of view, one which revealed my shame. Increasingly often, you could find me in this recovery scene; I could never seem to get ahead of the sinful scene. I hated myself. *Why do I become angry so easily? How can I not become angry at all? Lord, please help me!*

Each time when I came to my senses after the senseless fighting with my husband, my heart broke for my young son, Richard. I dropped to my knees, and with teary eyes, begged for forgiveness. More critically, I repented to God. I cried out to God desperately for forgiveness and for help not to repeat the same stupid thing.

Then one day, my ears were hearing our fighting again in the car. My husband was driving, and my children were in the backseat. Before I knew it, I happened to make him mad again, or maybe he had triggered me. Regardless, we were both out of control and yelling in fierce anger. Feeling thwarted and wanting to be helped desperately, I called out to God, like sending an SOS message for help from the depths of the sea of my heart.

Suddenly, I felt a tiny pat on my back about three times. I was alerted and looked back at my children and asked if either of them had patted me. They denied it strongly, opening their eyes wide and shaking their heads, being afraid of their mom. Then I lost my turn to yell back at my husband.

He earned a bonus chance to rebuke me twice in a row, at a higher pitch. Nonetheless, I was losing all of my turns to defend myself. Surprisingly, all my attention was swayed to only one thing. *What was that tiny tap or pat? Surely it was three times! Who did it? It was like a baby hand with a very light soft touch! Was it even more than a pat?*

Perplexed and pondering about it, I could perceive only a minuscule inner voice, "You can do it!" It was almost imperceptible, but it was definitely a voice, which was so sweet. It was the strangest thing and captured me at once from the deep sea. I lost the stormy argument with my husband. Once more, I had to confirm with my children about the patting. They denied it even stronger with their whole body language, defending themselves.

In that event, my husband became super victorious. He was beaming and whistling at his victory. Everything he stated at that moment did not matter to me in the slightest. It didn't bother me at all. He never knew how I was lost in awe, gleefully. In fact, I realized I let him win for the first time! I was amazed that I could yield to him. I had even felt a mysterious delight in myself that I was able to hold my anger and succumb to him. It wasn't a bad feeling at all to lose! I had even discovered a new power and strength in myself! Unbelievably, I truly felt much more victorious than him, with an unerasable grin on my face.

The feeling of patting didn't leave me for days. It was such a sweet and gentle touch; I never wanted it to fade away from my senses. Eventually, I had to acknowledge that it was the Holy Spirit who intervened for the first time in my life, and it was only the beginning. Honestly, there have been numerous times when it was still not easy to hear the Holy Spirit because the hurt was so strong, but the extent of our fighting gradually diminished to almost nothing. At least there was somebody who was crying out and seeking the Lord in the midst of the darkest valleys and stormy oceans and choosing to yield to God consistently. And God was faithful!

Joyce Meyer taught me that it requires only obedience for God to work in us and that obedience brings pain at first, and then delight comes later. This I can confirm. At times I wonder how I can be the same person when I recall my childhood. I went from depressed pessimist to cheerful optimist because of God's grace. He wrote my fairy tale! Regardless, I still fall short and slide back, but with God's help, I keep on moving forward in faith. Imagining how much more God can change me for His goodwill excites me!

There is a Korean proverb: "Men never change from age three to eighty." That's the world's belief that people don't change. But people in Christ Jesus keep being changed in unlimited capacity because of surrendering themselves to Him. That's why Scripture says: "Do not conform any longer to the pattern of this world, but be transformed by the renewing of your mind. Then you will be able to test and approve what God's will is — his good, pleasing and perfect will" (Romans 12:2).

Although my husband and I were devastated by spiritual warfare, my discernment over the years taught me that God was with us even then, and His invisible rod and staff protected us in the midst of the shadow of the dark valleys. He has never left us nor forsaken us through His unbelievable faithfulness. *Thank You, my Lord! I will praise Your name forever!*

My son, Richard, who was my first prayer partner, was saved at Creation Christian Music Festival at age 16. He has been serving at our church youth group since college. Presently, he is twenty-eight years old. He loves children and loves to counsel them. He told me that God has transformed all of his pain and hurt from the first decade of childhood into wisdom and an ability to understand others at a deeper level, to serve God by serving the youth.

My daughter, Ashley, twenty-three years old, who is my buddy and also a prayer partner, was a small group leader at Rutgers Intervarsity and served at Vacation Bible School at church.

I baptize you with water, but he will baptize you with the Holy Spirit.

Mark 1:8

His father Zechariah was filled with the Holy Spirit and prophesied.

Luke 1:67

And with that he breathed on them and said, "Receive the Holy Spirit."

John 20:22

Then Peter said, "Silver or gold I do not have, but what I do have I give you. In the name of Jesus Christ of Nazareth, walk."

Acts 3:6

And the disciples were filled with joy and with the Holy Spirit.

Acts 13:52

So, as the Holy Spirit says: "Today, if you hear his voice, do not harden your hearts as you did in the rebellion, during the time of testing in the wilderness, where your ancestors tested and tried me, though for forty years they saw what I did."

Hebrews 3:7–9

3. Breaking Free from Chains and Bondage

Above, the story of my first Holy Spirit encounter was focused on the event and description of my very first steps into spiritual growth. Below, this story is about the extensive process of finding my invisible chains and being set free from them.

Most people, while growing up, develop certain unique inclinations that shape their character. Some qualities are inherited; some qualities can be invisible to the observer, but they still guide that person's actions and feelings. If a person possesses a sunny disposition, that can inspire others; likewise, if his or her disposition is poor, that can negatively affect others and can even cause suffering. The invisible root of negative traits is spiritually recognized as chains and bondage. Unfortunately, most people do not recognize these destructive, all-consuming burdens. But God wants us to be set free!

From the very beginning and continuously, my marriage was not easy. There had been moments I felt obstructed by my husband, by the opposing forces within our personalities. There was a lack of unity within our marriage. The wall between us became thicker and higher.

I never knew that I was part of the problem to begin with, but later I learned that I had started my marriage while bringing in all of the chains and bondage I had accumulated throughout my early life. It is embarrassing to say that it took two decades (into my forties) to figure out my chains. However, I had never acknowledged them because I had never learned or investigated them until I started a Bible study of *Breaking Free* by Beth Moore in 2011. This study became the door for me to enter the promised land of freedom, a new beginning of spirituality, and the life God had prepared for me.

Through the scriptures and study, the Holy Spirit took me to where my chains and bondages were buried as deep wounds, never properly cared for, to be set free, one by one. This was accomplished not in a blaming way but in a tender, loving way. He poured and poured His shower of love on me and my wounds to be drenched and soaked. As I was healed through His unbelievable love, which is greater than all my problems, my chains melted away. In His pool of love, breaking free from all chains and any bondage was possible. God knew what I was going through and what I needed at that time in my life, and without His love, I wouldn't have been able to overcome it.

These were the chains I found in me.

Chain one: I had to admit that I hated men, all men. This perspective was developed throughout my childhood because of my father, who I thought had abandoned me and my mom. For the entire amount of my childhood, I had missed him. Because I missed him, I hated him. Thus, I hated all men. This affected my marriage and handicapped my ability to love my husband freely.

Chain two: I had a fear deep within me of being divorced. I knew my mom was divorced. I heard her sharing this with her priest when I was in second grade. I read my birth record repetitiously, and it triggered unbearable pain and resentment growing up. I did not discover my fear of being divorced until after it wreaked havoc on my marriage, until I found the special Bible study God had prepared for me. It was a hidden fear, buried deep within me, the possibility of being divorced by my husband. I was determined not to ever be divorced from my husband, so I lived in a state of anxiety, speculating his thoughts whenever we argued. Each time when my doubt was driven above the surface, I said I wanted to divorce him, blurting it out before he did: "Let's divorce." I had to win at the contest if we had to have one.

The two chains described above impacted my life considerably, especially during my first decade of marriage, before being born again spiritually. So, I repented and asked my husband to forgive me, kneeling on the floor.

Chain three: this chain was the longest and the heaviest, as I was damaged the most by my grandmother's abuse. It was mental and emotional, an unreasonable oppression that spanned my childhood. This experience caused me to become extremely stressed when encountering any higher authority. I was always afraid of my bosses: *what if I annoy them or I fail to please them?* Not only bosses but coworkers and guests. I felt I always had to please them, worrying whether they liked me. Uselessly, I proved myself by overworking, overthinking, and people-pleasing.

That was the same reason, in subsequent years, that I didn't want to listen to my husband or be submissive to him. I was determined to never allow anybody other than my grandmother to rule over me, at least not in my home. I became my own boss with a "don't rule me" attitude toward my husband. However, he wasn't an impressionable person. He valued the old-school standards, caring tremendously about what people thought about us. He always acted as if he belonged to the older generation, and I caved to follow him. I hated to do it. I had never had a good role model of a wife, not having heard or been taught to respect the husband even in and out of the church.

Chain four: I had lived with so much bitterness due to Grandmother's abuse. I had so much anger inside me, ready to erupt like a volcano at any unfair challenge against me, especially the challenge of my husband.

Outwardly, I could act well to look confident and happy because I had gained the ability to survive in my grandmother's house and to please her, but inwardly I had grown to become a card-carrying pessimist.

Guess what? My husband wasn't much better. He had carried his own baggage into our marriage as he also lacked a solid role model of a husband. No wonder we were like two mad cows butting into each other. He was only a churchgoer for the first decade of marriage—very faithful. Then, he slipped away due to all the trauma the Korean church had inflicted (he is soon-to-be-saved, in God's time).

For a long time, I questioned and blamed God for allowing us to marry, only to live as mismatched and miserable human beings on this earth. Surely we must be an impossible couple in the eyes of God!

So, what does this mean? How can I say that I've

been set free from chains and bondage? How did I become a different person from who I used to be? These are all similar and valid questions.

The process must have started immediately, following my born-again experience, but it wasn't trouble-free, and I wasn't changed overnight. There were countless days that I had wanted to give up and cried tears only God could measure.

Nevertheless, I never quit in the race of faith. Nothing stopped me from keeping my faith since I first called to Father God at age four or five. If the church produced a problem, I found another church. For me, it was a relationship unbreakable with God, regardless of all my iniquities and circumstances, because God was what I needed as a real, fatherless child. Father God filled that role for me from the moment I heard about Him.

My marriage was like living with the thorn that the Apostle Paul wanted removed from his life (2 Corinthians 12:7–8). I cried out to God millions of times about my husband, who had been so difficult since the beginning of marriage, that God would change him to be a better husband. I want no misunderstanding: he was perfectly acceptable out in the world, but as soon as he entered our home, he would transform into a noble from the Yi dynasty—stubborn, stressed, and in need of his servant. He didn't acknowledge how his actions contributed to our problems.

So far, God has molded me only. I chose to submit

to Him, and His hands molded me into a new but unfinished product. He is my potter; I am his clay (Jeremiah 18:6).

I must tell. The choice I had to make at the end of each trial, which was to be obedient to God's will, was not painless. Each time my flesh — my self-righteousness and pride — rather than wanting to die, fought with all its strength and might *against* God. At the time, there was maybe one percent of my flesh that wanted to do His will. Thus, I fell apart for innumerable reasons. It was completely impossible to think about the will of God during my spiritual infancy, at the foundation of my growing period, but God never gave up on me or my marriage.

In 2008, I did partial fasting for the first time, which I never wanted to do. I don't do diets, and I reasoned that my work was enough labor. Although it was only partial fasting, I experienced the power of it. When I cried out to God instead of feeding my flesh, despite the hunger pains, I felt something arising. My spirit, not my soul, was awakened from deep within me, and it yearned to do the will of God, which led me to the repentance of the sin I didn't know, which was some remaining hatred and negative feelings against my husband.

Fasting makes fleshly desires bow down to the Spirit, which only wants to do God's will and belongs to God. My experience affirmed what Pastor Franklin Jentzen preached and wrote about in his book, *Fasting*.

Since then, I willingly choose to fast to destroy and overcome my fleshly desire. I fast when I want to know His will better or whenever I have a special prayer request.

However, praising through music has become my number one activity, which greatly lifts me up anytime and with power almost equal to the fasting. No matter how hard life's challenges are, I turn on praise music, and it lifts me up. I have concert time frequently, blasting praise music everywhere: in my kitchen, in my car. Listening to it, I can both appreciate and accomplish all the housework I don't like.

Lastly, meditating on the word of God must be the most important and powerful, along with prayer. The Bible tells us that the word of God is our weapon to fight the enemy.

All these practices drew me closer to God, to be yoked together with Jesus, instead of donning the chains and bondage of my past. The ability was not even mine, to begin with. It was God's living power in me. Breaking my chains, I became set free because His word is living.

Therefore, mysteriously and gradually, I became able to yield and be submissive to my husband, who's as stubborn as a mule. It is unbelievable how much of a different wife I became to my husband, and I felt the encouragement from the Holy Spirit each time I faced an obstacle. *Oh, how the Holy Spirit encouraged me each time!* No matter how unpleasant or difficult things could seem, I was able to endure my pain by leaning on God. Before I knew it, yielding to my husband and surrendering my marriage to Him became a piece of cake, a joyful duty of my own free will. Most of all, I knew this was pleasing to God!

Although I'm still far from God's view, falling short at times since I wear this flesh, I will also never stop growing as His child, in His mercy and grace that follow me to eternity. It is written that His love and compassion simply never fail. They are new every morning. Great is His faithfulness (Jeremiah 23:8).

Last but not least, I can embrace peace and joy, which surpass all understanding — utilizing my given privilege — even though I suffer at times, as I choose to fix my eyes on Jesus (Hebrews 12:2). Where can I buy peace and joy such as this in this world?

As the result of the outpouring love of God, my choice of obedience to Him, and His hand-picked discipline courses, I have become who I am now, to tell everything, not in shame but in joy, humility, and honesty. Hallelujah!

My husband and I celebrated our thirtieth wedding anniversary recently. We have lived our last decade pretty peacefully and are now more peaceful than ever. Without God, it was impossible, and truly God makes the impossible possible (Matthew 19:26). I love my husband, who God gave to me! Amen! Hallelujah!

They will rebuild the ancient ruins and restore the places long devastated; they will renew the ruined cities that have been devastated for generations.

Isaiah 61:4

If only you had paid attention to my commands, your peace would have been like a river, your well-being like the waves of the sea.

Isaiah 48:18

Is not this the kind of fasting I have chosen: to loose the chains of injustice and untie the cords of the yoke, to set the oppressed free and break every yoke?

Isaiah 58:6

Take my yoke upon you and learn from me, for I am gentle and humble in heart, and you will find rest for your souls. For my yoke is easy and my burden is light.

Matthew 11:29–30

Therefore, there is now no condemnation for those who are in Christ Jesus, because through Christ Jesus the law of the Spirit who gives life has set you free from the law of sin and death.

Romans 8:1–2

Come near to God and he will come near to you. Wash your hands, you sinners, and purify your hearts, you double-minded.

James 4:8

Therefore, if anyone is in Christ, the new creation has come; The old has gone, the new is here!

2 Corinthians 5:17

4. The Word of God that Raised Me

It was 2003 when I was working as a nail tech in a salon. One day as I was serving my nail client, who was a college student, she told me that both of her parents were suffering from cancer. My heart sank for this young girl with empathy, thinking of my two young children, and I had no words to comfort her. However, she comforted me instead. She told me that she believed in God and wondered what great plans God prepared for her after all these trials. Her faith astonished me and caused me to drop my chin because I had never seen such genuine faith right in front of my eyes.

At the time, I was making only a tiny step into holiness, in my mid-thirties, after my recent born-again experience. So I couldn't believe how she possessed double the faith I had at her age, sounding so strong and mature as only a young college student. Remembering how I had been like a lost soul, a wanderer in the wilderness at her age, I felt embarrassed in my mind. I couldn't help but ask, almost demanding to know how she could have that much faith at her age, and she answered that she had graduated from a Christian school where she was educated with the word of God and praised Him. At that very sharp moment of listening to her, I felt as if lightning struck me, thinking I must send my son Richard to this school! A sudden desire was placed in my heart that Richard would possess this same wisdom as my client at an early age, which could give him the strength to face the world and its challenges.

Until then, I had never thought of private school for my children and thought even if I were wealthy, private school would be a luxury. When I came home from work that day, I fell on the floor straightforwardly and pleaded to God to guide me and grant that I could send my son to that Christian high school. Richard was in middle school at the time. After that prayer, God placed in me another sudden desire for a personal business that I had never wished for before but caused me to open up a nail salon the following year. Richard started to attend the school my client had graduated from the year after that.

At the time, I was attending an American church after I drifted away from the Korean churches I previously attended. I started a weekly, private Bible study in my nail salon as an answer to my prayers. This was planned *before* opening up my nail salon. I thought about starting a Bible study immediately after God planted in me the idea of a nail salon. The study was open for both my church friends and my other clients.

"Trust in the Lord with all your heart and lean not on your own understanding; in all your ways acknowledge him, and he will make your paths straight" (Proverbs 3:5–6).

This scripture verse challenged me endlessly. I memorized the verse above but continued to get stuck on the very first line. As soon as I recited it, I doubted my heart, knowing I wasn't *fully* trusting God. So then, how could I expect the rest to happen to me?

What I expected was that my business would be very successful as soon as it opened because it was God who gave me the desire to do it, but it wasn't. Instead, this business tested me time and again, which caused me to relinquish control and depend on God. I could do nothing without Him. It was a custom-made, intensive discipline course God had prepared specifically for me because God wanted to strengthen the coward inside me.

"With all your heart" was echoing into the layers of valleys in my soul. The faint echoes brought God's whisper back into my ears: "You are not trusting me yet." Every time I recited the verse, I felt that my heart was being measured up by God, so I tried to press and squeeze my heart to be presentable to God. Sensing the number on His scale was not indicating "full," I was just so frustrated like a child. Over and over, I had to cry out to God to help me overcome my unbelief. I felt anxious and worried in my heart, and that's not trusting God.

Nonetheless, I kept reciting it whenever and wherever I went and desperately prayed to God to make it happen. I knew my trusting would increase someday when I have less anxiety and more peace, but it was the opposite as my circumstance was not optimistic. This cycle went on for a good while as if I only went around in circles. However, I didn't give up and kept pressing toward it.

October 2011 was an extremely hopeless time. I closed my nail salon after about eight years of business. When I decided to close it, after being narrowed and cornered to the decision, I felt dreadful with thoughts like, *My life is over*, and *I'm a failure*, and it threw me into a deep endless pit. While being dumped and falling into a pit like a black hole in the space in my mind, I was trying hard to remember something floundering in the air: *God said He would never leave me nor forsake me! But how am I falling! God, help me! Help me to trust You!*

I shouted out to Him and grabbed the rope of the word of God with all my strength.

A few days after that day, after meeting my attorney for the matter of the lease of the business, I was driving on the highway reciting two other verses along with Proverbs 3:5–6. "God never leaves nor forsakes me" (Hebrews 13:5) was the first one. I had to grab all these verses tightly so as not to fall into a bottomless pit. And this is the verse I was reciting at the moment:

"Those who hope in the Lord will renew their strength. They will soar high on wings like eagles; they will run and not grow weary; they will walk and not be faint" (Isaiah 40:31).

I was driving on Route 130 reciting all those verses together, and suddenly I was lifted in the air, not physically, but I was lifted high with a soaring spirit! I felt I was soaring high on the wings of an eagle looking down at my vehicle. It was impossible that my body was still driving, but my soul and spirit soared as if I were flying high, and that was how I was made to believe on that day. One minute I was covered and dragged with fear and darkness, but the next minute, I was showered by the power of the Holy Spirit. All my fear was swept away, and only courage and confidence occupied me. Even overwhelming peace and joy burst inside of me, and I was laughing wildly. The whole world inside me was changed in seconds as if I had moved to a different dimension. I was in absolute peace! The presence of God is peace!

That is why my biggest goal in my faithful journey today is keeping my peace, no matter what! I have no idea how it happened, but it seemed like that I must have touched the border of trusting God when I pressed into loving and trusting Him with all my heart. It happened with the help of the Holy Spirit. The living word of God buried in the Bible becomes alive, and it lifts, swifts, tears down, and showers. It does unbelievable miracles as the petitioner believes in it with all of his or her heart.

Gradually, since experiencing unbelievably power-ful moments in my real life, trusting God has become easier. Once anybody experiences God's miracles (like unexplainable nonsense), then they get to learn to trust God, no matter how difficult the circumstances are, just like a little child, as simple and as possible.

So it has become God who has been the actual driver of my life, placing and removing my desires through the different seasons in my life, and that was the way He led me on the path He wanted me to be on. Sometimes there were seasons I was holding to, but I realized that without ending a season, the new season wouldn't come.

"Love the Lord your God with all your heart and with all your soul and with all your mind and with all your strength" (Mark 12:30).

When one of the teachers of the law asked Jesus what was God's greatest commandment, Jesus replied with the above verse. While I was reading the Bible, it penetrated my heart, and I started to memorize and meditate on it since it's the greatest commandment. However, as I recited it, I became only more anguished. It was impossible to be like that in this fast-paced, extra busy lifestyle we are living.

Oh, Lord, I'm busy working. I can't concentrate on You now, but You want me to love You with all my heart now!

Even with all my mind and soul and strength? That's impossible, God! How can I do that? Do You want me to work or not?

I was extremely bothered by this verse that God was demanding me to keep. *Why do You want me to love You so much like that? I love You, God; You know that I do. But that's not enough, right? Wow, You truly want me to love You much more than I can do now! Fully and completely? With all my heart, with all my mind, with all my soul, and with all my strength! Oh, wow! How will I be able to do all that? How? When?*

Each time I tried, but I ended up being only more frustrated and started to think something like this: *Oh, God, what's wrong with You? Why do You want to be loved by me so much? Then I can't do anything else while I only try to love You so completely! Why do You demand something I cannot do?*

Nonetheless, on and off, I guess I tried to think of Him more often, even during my work and at any challenging moment, with extra verses. One such verse was "The Lord is my shepherd, I shall not want" (Psalm 23:1), which comforted me immediately as I recited it.

The time I had my nail salon business (2004–2011) was the first decade after being born-again, and it could be summed up as the worst spiritual warfare of all, including my home situation—husband, young children, and my mom. In this period, I had no choice but to stick with God and grow spiritually so that I could survive the storms in my life.

Later what God revealed to me was that His love, which is living in me through the love that I made in my heart, is working back for all my benefit. Simply, His love converted into the purest and most potent painkiller for my soul, numbing all the pain this world threw at me. Over and over, His love, living in me, became activated like a shield against all the forces of spiritual warfare in this dark place and like a fireproof against fires in the bombarding battlefield of life.

More and more, I perceived that even when I still felt the pain and even when I was still crying devastatingly, wondering where God was, God carried me through in His loving arms. I just could not know all this before because I didn't even remember what He did for me, similar to how our children don't remember anything their parents did for them when they were little.

The greatest commandment for loving God wasn't about His selfishness. It wasn't His ego. It wasn't that God lacked our love. All of His commandments are not for His needs but for ours. He knew we wouldn't be able to live this life without His love.

To conclude, my discovery about the greatest commandment is that He reveals how He loves us and why we desperately need His love, which leads and enables us to love our neighbors as ourselves. He knows us best!

This is why I can say that the word of God rescued

and raised me to be the woman who I am today! Thank You, my Father, my God!

Even youths grow tired and weary, and young men stumble and fall; but those who hope in the LORD will renew their strength. They will soar on wings like eagles; they will run and not grow weary, they will walk and not be faint.
Isaiah 40:30–31

Oh, how I love your law! I meditate on it all day long.
Psalm 119:97

Your word is a lamp for my feet and a light on my path.
Psalm 119:105

Great peace have those who love your law, and nothing can make them stumble.
Psalm 119:165

5. My Hands and Miracles

Part 1

It was past midnight, April 2012. I was jolted from my sound sleep with a sharp, stabbing pain. Some part of me was burning, but I didn't know what it was! Eyes still closed, I sensed for where the pain was originating. I couldn't move my hands well. I opened my eyes: my hands! They looked so big, much bigger than my ordinary hands. They couldn't be my hands. They were so huge, even in the darkness. They looked like the hands of the Hulk!

What was this transformation? *Is this real life, or am I still in my dream?* My hands felt so stiff. I could not clench or close them. They were like thick tree branches! It was impossible to stretch them the way I like to stretch my fingers.

This had to be a nightmare! I wanted to scream, but I blocked my mouth so as not to wake up my husband.

Unbelievably, this was happening in real life, and furthermore, this wasn't the first time. I had been granted a miracle once before. That was four months ago, and it should never have happened again. At that time, I believed there had been a miracle because I had asked for it.

I recall my experience from that first time, in December of 2011: although the fear attacked me, I cried out to God immediately. *Oh no, Lord, help me! Help me, my Father! What happened to my hands? Heal my hands! I have to work today. You know that my job is to work with my hands! Cure my hands! Oh, Almighty Father!*

Father, You know my situation. What else can I do? I have been a nail tech, and this is all I know and the only thing I can do well. I still have to work with my hands for twenty more years.

Oh no, Lord Jesus, You said everything is possible with You! Nothing is impossible for You (Philippians 4:13). Oh, Mighty Lord, do something for me!

But poor me, I was filled with fear, worry, and doubt, wondering if I could work that day. *And what time was my first appointment? Should I cancel for today? Oh, will it be better by tomorrow?*

My alarm beeped. It was one of the longest nights; I was afraid of the morning. Morning awaited me with no mercy or flexibility, as usual, with its duties just the same. Two people need my hands to help start their day: my husband and my daughter.

First, I wanted to be strict with myself, just moving a little slowly, but I couldn't manage anything right. I was helpless. Being unable to do my regular routine with my hands, I felt afraid. Nevertheless, one thing I could not give up was praying. I was forcing myself to pray earnestly that the Lord would do something for me. The real question was, would I trust Him?

I must trust if He is looking at me now. There is no other choice but to trust Him. If I trust Him now, I know it has to be with all my heart!

Oh Lord, please! Are You looking at me now? Are You listening to me? Please, Lord, fix my hands! I'm desperate, Lord! O Lord, You know I have only You! Who else can I ask?

This will be only a test, a simple test; it will go away soon!

I remembered that if I allowed myself to doubt my prayers, then I would only be double-minded. That doubting person should not believe that he will receive anything (James 1:6–8).

Oh no, my unbelief! Oh Lord, help me overcome my unbelief, I pleaded (Mark 9:24).

I was thrown into a battlefield to fight against this very unbelief within my mind. I felt that two sides torn apart within me were fighting against each other.

My husband (soon-to-be-saved) was getting ready for work, and he heard me talking about my hands, so he worried a little for me. However, I was remaining calm for him until he left that morning at the normal time because I knew he did not really have any room to worry about anything other than himself, a poor thing, so bound by himself and his job.

I thanked God for my husband's undertaking of the family as a faithful supporter, but I prayed for him to get to know there is somebody else supporting him who has his back. If he could just trust his "wife's God" and leave his burdens to Him, then his life would be changed.

It's God who is in control, not me or my husband, and the Almighty keeps everything going for us. So I choose to press on. *I have to pass this test of trusting God. Nothing hinders me, Lord, nothing.*

It was now my daughter's turn: I am her chauffeur daily. We send her to a Christian high school, a private school with no bus service. The drive is about a half-hour one way. I had no choice but to drive her, but I could not grip the wheel right. Painfully, I barely gripped the wheel. It was as if I wore a huge bubble-shaped mitten, which didn't allow me to grip anything tightly enough.

At the time, I was working part-time as a freelance nail technician after ending my salon business only a month ago. Due to this, my workload had decreased significantly, and I could be more flexible with my time and my schedule. Fortunately, my nail appointments started later that morning, not earlier. Thank God! I started to feel slightly better toward midday, hour by hour, bit by bit. Slowly recovering, I felt I was at about three-quarters of my best. Thank God I'm a professional; I was still able to manage the work. I put forth all my effort not to show my discomfort or be noticed by anyone. All of my personal clients are like my friends, and I especially didn't want them to worry about me. I didn't want them to feel any added stress on my behalf. Anyway, I blocked my schedule for a lighter workload.

I never ceased praying that it was only a one-day attack and it would not come back. I was thanking

God that the long day of work was over, but now my hands were rapidly worsening toward evening and midnight. This was the scariest thing! I felt like I was caught in some kind of spell by the enemy.

But I have Jesus! Mighty One! In the name of Jesus, I was fighting it with my spiritual warfare. At the same time, I kept thinking about what I should do. I tried to do some light acupuncture therapy at home that night with a small tool that my mom uses when she has joint pain. Previously, it had given me great results on my knee, shoulder, and ankle. So I had a pretty strong hope for it, but it didn't do anything this time. The fear attacked me again: I cried out to God and believed He would give me a miracle! Nonetheless, the same symptoms were appearing on my hands, day and night. I was still doing more acupuncture therapy, plus melted paraffin on my hands again, but nothing was effectively working. I had to do something as I was determined to make it better.

One evening I was sitting on the bathroom floor dipping my hands in a bucket of paraffin. It is a warm-hot liquid wax that makes our skin soft and moisturized. Paraffin treatment was already well known as a very good solution for helping any type of arthritis condition. Most people love to do paraffin treatment for the softening of hands and instant deep warmth for their body, especially in a cold winter season.

But it's not heard of to be using paraffin like I did

for my inflated hands. I felt like I was under some kind of cruel punishment. My body was soaking with sweat from dipping my hands for half an hour, while normally, you are only meant to dip for just seconds. It didn't do anything. I continued for an hour, and yet, nothing changed.

I kept wondering whether or not I should make an appointment with the doctor. *What procedures will it take to find out what's wrong with me? How much time will it take? When would I be cured, and can I even be cured completely? What medicine can cure this sort of thing, and what side effects will there be?* I've heard from my clients many times how it takes forever just to be diagnosed correctly.

Nevertheless, I never stopped praying while I was attempting all the remedies I knew: doing acupuncture therapy, using paraffin at midnight, working during the day, eating, walking, etc., as I kept crying out to the Lord. Then, after exactly seven days, God granted me my miracle. My hands were cured immediately, completely. I never went to a doctor and didn't use any medicine.

Part 2

The nightmare sprung again after just four months, on April 14, 2012. It came back again without any warnings. No symptoms! *What could I do?* I cried out to God immediately.

It was only three days after my husband and I started praying together for the first time in our married life, and right after I made one great praise report in my small Bible study group. It came the exact same way at midnight. I was scared when I looked at my huge, swollen, burning hands, but my first thought scared me more: *This is it! There are no more miracles! It was just a one-time special. Don't even think about it a second time! You will have to live with it!*

Immediately I felt myself falling into an endless dark hole, and while I was falling, I was trying to remember something: *His promise! For Jesus, anything and everything is possible. Nothing is impossible! I will still ask for His miracle!*

I sprang up out of it so speedily. I realized that the scary thoughts were only the enemy's lies and deception to trick me into not asking for the miracle ever again. Here, my battle started anew.

A couple of days later, I kept on praying despite being down. In the background, I heard my mom talking about something, something about lemons. The monthly Korean health magazine she always reads talked about lemon research, and, apparently, it could help her light case of asthma. So I bought some lemons for her at the grocery store.

Then, the next minute she made me read the line that said, "lemon with the peel prevents and cures rheumatism and arthritis."

I thought, *Okay, why not try it?* The saying goes, "When life gives you lemons, make lemonade," right?

I started to add a slice of lemon peel to my home-made, blended smoothie. Meanwhile, I canceled some nail appointments here and there in that week for the first time in my career. Although I was down a little, I kept eating my fair share of lemon peels and asking for a miracle. Most of all, I pressed deeply into prayer to God to help me trust Him. I still thought about medical procedures, wishing and praying that I could stretch my hands and arms all the way out, over and above my head, the way I loved to every day. *Oh, how I wished to fully stretch, properly, all the way!*

Exactly seven days after I started taking these lemon peels, God granted me a miracle for the second time on April 23, 2012. I was able to stretch my hands all the way to their maximum flexibility! Exactly after seven days.

This time it happened through lemons! It was unbelievable! I didn't do anything but eat the lemon peels. Rarely had I added lemons to our family's nutrition. We didn't like lemons much before, but not anymore. *Lemons! Who would think of eating the skin or peel of a lemon? How could a monthly magazine come at just the right time? How could it carry such lemon research? How could my mom find out about it at exactly the time I needed it?* Even the number of days, seven days for each miracle, was very interesting. It matched God's special number of days for creation.

The article on lemon research also said that the peel or skin prevents and cures many cancers and blood-related diseases too. All I had was my experience with lemons and this miracle that God granted to me. Whatever it may be, I was cured. So I started to tell everybody about my miracle experience with lemons.

Once, my pastor, retired Reverend David Mazzella, preached in a Sunday sermon that we refer to some junk as "lemons." If something is defective with a major flaw, we call it a lemon. There are even lemon laws whereby people can return their "lemons." Someone among us whom we really dislike can be referred to as a "lemon." We all have one or two "lemons" in our lives. Since we, as human beings, are so incomplete, from God's point of view, we can technically be considered "lemons" to God. My pastor even made us turn to look at the person sitting next to us and say, "I'm a lemon." It was hilarious!

Pastor Mazzella went on: while we are all "lemons" in a certain sense, God gave His only begotten Son, Jesus, to die on the cross for our sins to save us for eternity. And God does perform miracles with us "lemons," too.

My hands are not ordinary hands to me anymore. I am looking at and checking them as often as I can, in awe. God is whispering to me through my hand, "I am with you." Truly He is the God of miracles!

Part 3

Sometimes I experience a dramatic change in my body that I have no control over. The mood swings affected by certain hormones in the human body make me feel nothing but vulnerable. I do not welcome that feeling, but this new feeling has no leash. It is so dominating. *Why do I feel so sad and miserable, suddenly, when I wake up?* It was on Monday morning only after the Lord's blessed day just yesterday. These sudden mood swings seemed like an unforeseen thunderstorm after a great sunny day in my body. This doesn't happen only to me, but to every woman I talk to, including my daughter, who goes through it from time to time. I don't know about men, but women go through this more frequently, regardless of our desire. Actually, we don't plan this.

One morning, I felt particularly gloomy and heavy on my drive to work, so I turned on my music for my daily remedy — but desperately at the time, to lift me up. *Please, God! Please!* I chose Chris Tomlin's new CD, *Never Lose Sight*, and I picked this one song, "Impossible Things," which has the fastest, most uplifting beat of the album, so it could eradicate the gloomy, awful feeling I was suffocated by on that morning. Despite that I love all the songs, I choose to listen to certain songs from the album over and over because I like to be stuck with certain songs depending on my mood.

You heal the broken hearted

You set the captive free
You lift the heavy burden
And even now, You are lifting me

Though I walk through the valley
Darkness surrounding me
There You prepare a table, hmm-hmm
In the presence of my enemies, yeah-eh[3]

Somehow the beat of this song sounded so sweet, and the tapping rhythm was like a familiar warm comfort patting on my shoulder. My body was giving in to following the rhythm. In the middle of the song, Chris Tomlin's friend kicked in this line: "Though I walk through the valley, darkness surrounding me, there You prepare a table, hmm-hmm, in the presence of my enemies!"

Chris Tomlin kindly invites his friends to contribute to his song tracks. Anyway, Danny Gokey sang that line, but how can he sing it so merrily? Being irritated at his style, I wanted to talk with him: *Hello! That is the darkest valley you are walking in, and you go through it as care-free! How can you do it? You say you walk through the valley of darkness. It is so heavily dark there, but you walk through it happily like Tigger from* Winnie the Pooh?

I couldn't believe the way he sang it, almost annoy-

3 "Impossible Things," featuring Danny Gokey, MP3 audio, track 3 on Chris Tomlin, *Never Lose Sight*, sixstepsrecords/Sparrow Records, 2016.

ingly!

However, the very next line had a dramatic twist: "There You prepare a table in the presence of my enemies." It sounded unbelievable what God does! But honestly, I wondered about that *table*. I had never thought about it until then. *What does that mean?* I kept repeating the song, only that part, over and over, imagining what kind of table it could be. *Is it a table of food? Will it be a feast?* Vaguely I assumed that God will surprise us in His special way if we suffer well coming out of the darkest valleys in our lives.

Then I discerned why Danny Gokey can bounce like Tigger. He is confident that God will meet him at the end of that valley and surprise him in an amazing way! He was bouncing there like a little child, excitedly trusting and expecting God! I was astonished at his demeanor. In the next second, we sang in harmony.

Some minutes ago, I was facing a giant in the four-sided square box of my mind. There was somebody huge, looking like a champion, wearing a brilliant champion belt, and there I was thrown in the ring with him, circling fearfully around him toward the edge. As I was listening to every verse of the song, pressing into each one, there was a magnificent victory, won before even I knew it. My gigantic champion, a Goliath, was lying down in front of me, completely helpless. My confidence came back!

The next morning, a Tuesday, my small group sang

"Impossible Things" with the CD player. I shared my high and low of the week with the group. I shared how God worked with that particular song for me yesterday. I thought my high and low report was finished there, but it was not.

> *Even though I walk through the darkest valley,*
> *I will fear no evil, for you are with me; your rod*
> *and your staff, they comfort me.*
> **Psalm 23:4**

Part 4

Tuesday passed into Wednesday in November 2017. I was sleeping well until a heavy pressure was against me and woke me up. It was about 2 a.m. I was drenched with sweat, and I saw my hands were gigantic! My hands were unfoldable! It was horrifying. My body was shivering with fear despite the fact that my husband was snoring right next to me. The air was so chilly in my room. That giant from the square boxing ring of my mind had returned. *How can this happen again? It was so long ago. I have been so well. Oh, God! Come and rescue me!*

I knelt down at my bedside. Somehow from the song that had been stuck in my brain for a couple of days, the lyrics started to play in me automatically. *I'm thrown into this valley once again. The darkest valley. And I must walk through it. How will I walk?*

My tears streamed down. *I'm not alone! His rod and staff comfort me!* I bit my lip and asked myself, *Will I walk out defeated or victorious?*

The song kept playing in my head. *Oh, God! You prepared me with this song! You knew this would happen to me. You gave me this song in advance to support me.* I swallowed all my fear and doubt at once: I was determined.

"Enemy, you feeble thing, get away from me. I'm not afraid of you. I believe God will prepare a table for me in front of you! He surely will! You will see how He does it!" I declared it to the enemy.

Reciting Psalm 23 and Isaiah 41:10, I started to pray to the Almighty, my Father. As I prayed to God for a table that He would prepare for me, my head was filled by God with the faces of the members of my small group. Suddenly I was praying on behalf of each and every one of them, not for me—and I was crying out for them, feeling their pain as if it was mine. I had prayed for others before, many times, but not in this way, sobbing and wailing from midnight to dawn. Everyone in my group was going through some dark valley in her own life. Nobody's prayer request was less than anybody else's. Everybody was aching and heavily burdened in that particular season.

Before I knew it, Wednesday morning settled in, and my hands looked terrible. I realized I wasn't faithful because I hadn't used the lemon peel remedy shown to me by God years ago. It was my own failure. I had neglected to remember God's miracle. How lazy and foolish I had been. There was nothing or nobody to blame. I repented.

Although I was down a little, I trusted God, who I knew well, to prepare the table. Strangely, this time, I wasn't asking for a miracle. Maybe I did, but I was so focused on the table. *What table is He preparing for me? What will it look like?* My curiosity was growing, and I couldn't wait to find out.

Before starting the day — it was my day off, thank God — I decided to take pictures of my swollen hands as a future reminder. I checked my emails for the day. Then an email (from someone with whom I had previously exchanged a couple of business emails) drew my attention. I believe the Holy Spirit hand-delivered that email to me. *Reply! Tell her about her Savior.*

I had never written an email like that to someone who was technically a stranger, but I followed my inner voice. I sent her a paragraph about who my Savior is and how He loves me and how He is for her. Jesus loves her so much as His beloved lost child! Perhaps she needed it urgently. As I clicked the send button, I felt relief and peace.

Meanwhile, I took extra good care of myself, consuming all the beneficial nutrients for my symptoms: lemon peel, ginger, turmeric, olive oil, omega-3 oil, vitamin D, etc.

Throughout the week, the Holy Spirit was encouraging me to share the gospel with whoever He entrusted to me. I was definitely more courageous than at any other time to follow His will, waiting for His table. I shared the gospel with all my nail clients that week. It was an unusually light workload that week. Even some appointments were canceled. Now Suzanna was the only one left.

Suzanna was my beloved client for a long time but the hardest one to share the gospel with. Although I had the urge to share with her many times, it seemed there was a high wall between us that I could never scale due to our religious differences. She was Jewish. It was midday on a Friday, the condition of my hands was manageable, still 65–75 percent, and they felt only mild discomfort when Suzanna came. I showed her the worst picture of my hands and told her that God wanted me to share this important news with her: "Beloved Suzanna, I can tell you this now, with extra special courage that God pours in me. I prayed to God specifically for a miracle for my hands. So I must totally trust in Him, and I do now."

"Jesus is the Son of God who became the perfect Lamb of God, spotless and sinless, to be the sacrifice for all our sins so that God washes us with His blood. And God raised Him on the third day, and He is living. It was the one and perfect sacrifice as the Son of God, which can cover all our sins for all whoever believes in Him and which also fulfilled all the prophecies in the Old Testament. So we are saved by faith, by believing in Him, and that is the grace of God. As a gentile myself, without Jesus, I never had hope, but I found hope in Him." I was breathless and didn't know how I said it.

Suzanna didn't jump out of her seat but stayed rather calm. She didn't frown or anything. I said I was sorry and thanked her for listening.

On Saturday, wow, my hands were almost back to normal, 80–90 percent, and pretty comfortable. The symptoms were disappearing much more quickly than before. As I was scheduled, I went to a nursing home ministry that afternoon, and I donated all the hand lotion I kept for my business to all the residents and people who served in our ministry. I had decided earlier in the week to give these products away.

On Sunday, when I showed my hands to my friends at my church describing what had happened during the week, nobody seemed to believe it because my hands looked fine. If I didn't have the proof of pictures, nobody would understand me. This time my hands were cured so rapidly, and it took the shortest time, not even five days.

On Monday, I went to my doctor for an appointment for my hands for the first time since the symptoms first occurred in 2011. This was after my hands had gotten better completely. I just wanted to hear what my doctor had to say. She said I should have come right away when the symptoms appeared, but at that point, it was all gone, and there was nothing she could find. Anyway, I had an X-ray taken, and it didn't show any problems.

On Tuesday, I went back to my small group. It seemed like it had been a long time ago, but only a week had passed. Proudly, I could present everything that had happened since last week and how God prepared a table for me in the presence of my enemies. Without showing pictures of my hands, I couldn't convince some to believe. All my symptoms indicated that it was rheumatoid arthritis, an aggressive and severe case.

The table that God prepared for me — in the late autumn of 2017 — in front of my enemies consisted of the following steps: my heartfelt prayers for every individual of my group, sharing the Gospel to my clients, sharing the Gospel to Suzanna, sharing the Gospel to a stranger through email, donating hand lotion at a nursing home, adding one more testimony of my own, deepening my faith.

Enemies attack us at times, but God provides the way out (1 Corinthians 10:13). He even prepares tables for us in front of them (Psalm 23:5).

For the last three years, my hands have been great, exhibiting no swelling. God kept allowing me to work with them. However, I know I have to be faithful to take care of myself. I have some stiffness at night, but with heavenly medicine, it is well under control.

God has been so good at taking care of me since I have others to take care of. He is awesome and so faithful, knowing my other daily burdens!

> *That's my Father!*
> *"I have never stopped loving you!"*
> *Oh, yes God, I know!*
> I laugh with delight in His goodness!

Even though I walk through the darkest valley, I will fear no evil, for you are with me; your rod and your staff, they comfort me. You prepare a table before me in the presence of my enemies. You anoint my head with oil; my cup overflows.
Psalm 23:4–5

So do not fear, for I am with you; do not be dismayed, for I am your God. I will strengthen you and help you; I will uphold you with my righteous right hand.
Isaiah 41:10

No temptation has overtaken you except what is common to mankind. And God is faithful; he will not let you be tempted beyond what you can bear. But when you are tempted, he will also provide a way out so that you can endure it.
1 Corinthians 10:13

The Most Extraordinary Season of My Life[4]

The Spirit of the Sovereign LORD is on me, because the LORD has anointed me to proclaim good news to the poor. He has sent me to bind up the brokenhearted, to proclaim freedom for the captives and release from darkness for the prisoners, to proclaim the year of the LORD's favor and the day of vengeance of our God, to comfort all who mourn, and provide for those who grieve in Zion—to bestow on them a crown of beauty instead of ashes, the oil of joy instead of mourning, and a garment of praise instead of a spirit of despair. They will be called oaks of righteousness, a planting of the LORD for the display of his splendor. They will rebuild the ancient ruins and restore the places long devastated; they will renew the ruined cities that have been devastated for generations.

Isaiah 61:1–4

Instead of your shame you will receive a double portion, and instead of disgrace you will rejoice in your inheritance. And so you will inherit a double portion in your land, and everlasting joy will be yours. For I, the LORD, love justice; I

---

4 To readers: the last portions of Chapters 1–4 happened within the last two to three years, and as such, are also considered part of my "Extraordinary Season."

hate robbery and wrongdoing. In my faithfulness I will reward my people and make an everlasting covenant with them. Their descendants will be known among the nations and their offspring among the peoples. All who see them will acknowledge that they are a people the Lord has blessed.

Isaiah 61:7–9

The book of Isaiah is part of the Old Testament of the Bible and was written by the Prophet Isaiah during 701–681 BC. After about 700 years from the time of Prophet Isaiah, Jesus entered the synagogue in Nazareth and read Isaiah chapter 61, verses 1 and 2. Then He said, "Today this scripture is fulfilled in your hearing" (Luke 4:16–21).

1. A Voyage to My Home Church

In the autumn of 2008, I fasted for ten days for the first time in my life. Even though it was only a partial fast, it was an elephantine decision to me. I had never tried a diet in my life, and hunger pain was the most irritating feeling! Additionally, my daily work was physical and included many pedicures, which require a lot of energy. I needed to eat, and the term "fasting" was novel to me. But God bestowed me with something almost indescribable my first time fasting.

To provide context, it was like heaven on earth. For a few days, consistently, I experienced perfect peace and joy like ecstasy. It was as if I walked on clouds. I felt I was surrounded by invisible shields from head to toe. I couldn't feel any of the ordinary stress or attacks from people at my business (even though I was surrounded by people and people were demanding, as usual). It was never because my fasting skills or efforts were tremendous, but because it was the very first fasting, willingly done from my heart and with repentance, that God lavished me with a big prize! Thus, it was the perfect timing of God meant to rescue me from the devastating depression I faced.

Once I experienced the power of fasting, I became hooked on fasting. Whenever I faced my weakness or needed His special guidance, I eagerly turned to fasting. Then, in the autumn of 2009, after spending a year growing spiritually, suddenly I found this thought in my heart that this past year had been the best year of my life. Nothing significant happened; my present prayers were not answered. Yet, I remember announcing this to my children ecstatically. Because I was really excited when I looked back, even from that point! I perceived that my life was transformed beyond measure from my youth, and I was thankful!

For the first time and in earnest, I sincerely thanked God for how He had led me, bringing me out of my

Egypt. I was no longer enslaved. My Egypt was my childhood at my grandmother's. There was no hope, only continual oppression and pain. I totally forgot about how I used to live. Without God, I could never be free from it, and He even set me free from all my shame.

Despite that God didn't answer my prayers during childhood, I found one great benefit out of it. The roots of my thankfulness extend deeper. Every time I lay on my bed, I release my soul into a more profound comfort, and I'm thankful that I'm not at my grand-mother's house. It may sound awkward, but I become so relieved when thinking on my bed, *Thank God! I'm in my house and not in my grandmother's!* It soothes like a personal lullaby.

When I shared this with my pastor's wife — she was my friend — she invited me to be the second speaker at the Annual Women's Dinner coming up in December 2009. It was such an honor to me personally for a couple of reasons. This would be my first time sharing my testimony in front of a large audience. Furthermore, the event was occurring in the American church I had attended for some years, which added pressure and significance for me because I had only attended Korean churches prior to going there.

To make a long story short, I was thrown out of the very same church by my pastor and his wife the following spring. It happened so quickly because of one honest confession to the pastor that I happened to read his email, which was forwarded to my son Richard from his friend.

When Richard's friend called him to say her family would no longer be coming to our church because the pastor had written to her dad saying he was a fool, Richard refused to believe it. That was why she forwarded the email to him. Both my children were shocked. *Surely there must be a communication problem, and it must be a huge mistake!* I felt a thump in my heart, but my first response to my children about the email was, "But…but we have to go to our church." It was a reactive and self-protecting thought.

When I turned around from my children, I was confronted by my conscience: *Will I be able to look at the pastor, pretending that I know nothing? On second thought,* I shook my head; *I cannot do it.* Most of all, because Richard's friend's family was like family to us. Her mom was my friend. This couple had been dedicated to hosting a youth group Bible study for years, which Richard enjoyed attending both within and outside of their home. They ran the study without support from the church. Then suddenly, the pastor decided to regulate all church activities enforcing hasty, stringent policies meant to fortify the system. These changes countermanded normal procedures.

I couldn't sleep at all, so I had to call the pastor the next morning to confess about reading the email as if I were confessing sins to the Father at Catholic church (I used to do that when I was young). Somewhat timidly, I confessed it saying, "I'm really sorry," while stuttering the whole time like a guilty person. And I finished, very carefully, with "Again, I'm so sorry. Is there anything I can do to help in this situation? Is it possible to reconcile with them?"

As I said this, my pastor's tone of voice over the phone was transformed into something I couldn't recognize, from gentle and sweet to angry and disgusted. A tone I had never heard from him until then. He spoke just like an angry man: "There is no change because everybody must follow the church rules, designed to protect the church congregation." He kept saying that he could not be driven by one person who was not listening while the church was growing rapidly. Then he said he highly recommended that *I* go to another church and another pastor. I cried out, "Oh my goodness, how can you say that?" Before I had even processed what I heard, "Goodbye." Done. It was over.

I was hit by an electric shock. Then I was shaky, and I burst out with a loud cry, screaming in my room. After an hour of crying, I couldn't believe what I had heard; I truly doubted my ears and memory, so after praying, I wrote an email to my pastor pleading the same thing. He sent me the same thing he had said to me on the phone. The only difference was now I received a written confirmation: "I highly recommend that Michelle Kim go to another church and find another pastor." I cried and wailed as if I'd just heard of the unexpected death of a friend. I had a funeral in my heart for my beloved pastor, whom I had loved and respected for years.

Until that day, my children and I were in love with our pastor, congregation, and church. When I reported this news to my children, we all squalled as if we were at a funeral. Richard was a freshman in college, and Ashley was an eighth-grader. However, we cried out to God to help us to forgive. While crying, I was also worrying: *What if my husband knew about this?* He stopped going to church with us after the last Korean church. I prayed that my husband had not known about this. I learned later that there were others who were also asked to leave by the pastor.

During the week, I had a nightmare, which rarely happens. In my dream, I happened to visit the pastor's church rather fearfully. Right before entering the sanctuary, some of my friends came and stopped me, saying, "Michelle, you are not allowed to come here anymore!"

On the following Sunday, we could have skipped going to church, not knowing where we should go. However, Richard received a suggestion from his friend, and we traveled to this unknown church by way of MapQuest. It was good to sit in a service again. We were not prohibited from attending *this* service, but we were sobbing, nonetheless, from the massive hurt we were still feeling. After the service, Richard asked me what my decision was. I said I didn't know: my heart was numb. So, we attended again next week, still not sure of anything.

On the third Sunday, I cried out to God, praying out loud so that my children could pray with me about what *He* wanted us to do and where we should go. I cried the entire way to church (the church recommended to Richard). The crying waned as I pulled into the parking lot. As I turned off my engine, I gazed up to the sky and prayed as if looking for the answer. I finished with "Amen" and watched the clouds move slowly in the most beautiful blue April sky. Suddenly, I heard a voice from somewhere, through the slowly passing clouds, a voice that spoke right into my ear and my mind. Each word was crystal clear, and time seemed to stop. The voice sounded so gentle, even called me by name.

"Michelle, everything is passing; nothing is everlasting. Only the glory of God is everlasting. Nothing is staying."

The voice was soft but firm and faded away slowly as the cloud floated away. It stunned me frozen, but I knew I heard the clear voice of God so comforting and so confirming. It made me spring out of my car's seat and call to my children cheerfully, "This is it. This is our church. We don't go anywhere else. God brought us here. Hallelujah!"

Now tears of joy streamed down my cheeks during the service, and most surprisingly, I watched a baptism ceremony for the first time that day. At the moment I was watching the baptism ceremony, I heard the sweet voice which talked to me from the clouds again: "You missed it. You need it." Therefore, I signed up immediately and had my baptism, in my church, at the very next baptism ceremony. Richard was baptized the following year, and then Ashley did it the year after Richard.

What had happened at the previous church was critically painful, but I discerned that it was God who used the whole situation to bring us to a church body and spiritual environment that was better suited for us. God always knows what's best for us!

Come to think of it, and it took a long time to find my home church. I have had to travel beyond my childhood, across the ocean, and through many deserts. I always enter my church with a grateful heart. It always makes my family laugh to think about how we came here that very first Sunday, by way of a MapQuest link, not even knowing the name of the church.

He says, "Be still, and know that I am God; I will be exalted among the nations, I will be exalted in the earth."

Psalm 46:10

I cried out to God for help; I cried out to God

to hear me.

Psalm 77:1

I lift up my eyes to the mountains—where does my help come from? My help comes from the LORD, the Maker of heaven and earth.

Psalm 121:1–2

Call to me and I will answer you and tell you great and unsearchable things you do not know.

Jeremiah 33:3

And we know that in all things God works for the good of those who love him, who have been called according to his purpose.

Romans 8:28

For the kingdom of God is not a matter of eating and drinking, but of righteousness, peace and joy in the Holy Spirit.

Romans 14:17

2. Excitement Even Without Good News (October 2018)

Entering this fall, I sense something unusual in me. Surprisingly, my complaints about my daily life have been greatly reduced in my heart. Though nobody knows about it, since it's the heart's concern, God must know it, and it must be by the help of the Holy Spirit.

But still, honestly, I must admit I deal with some vague, grouchy feelings rising from within me, especially during my housework since I'm the one who is mostly responsible for it. Indeed, I've been preparing meals for five, even two to three kinds of different dishes due to different cravings. I can't leave anyone unhappy. I keep telling my family that I don't run a cafeteria, but they keep telling me what they like to eat. Consequently, I end up being very tired and lacking personal time at the end of the day. Additionally, Mom was sick with pneumonia in the summer. She was hospitalized for half a month and now lives with oxygen tubes and BiPAP at night time, so I feel as if I am running a rehab home for her too.

I can laugh remembering the moment God spoke to me so personally about my housework a few years ago. It was when I was talking to Him in my head — roughly, with only complaining — about my housework while dishwashing. *This is nonsense! This is so much — endless. I can't do this anymore! What do You think, God? Don't You think this is too much? Why is my family so demanding? Isn't this impossible for a person to bear?* Then suddenly, a different voice than mine spoke to me very deeply in my heart, like an echo, "I didn't send you far. Didn't you want to serve me? Serve them here for me!" I knew then it was God. At His voice, I dropped whatever was in my hands in the sink; my jaw joined in astonishment. The water from the faucet was still running. His voice never rebuked me but sounded sweet, compelling even. I wanted to hear more. I couldn't believe He met me even at my ugliest.

I know I can never be perfect as long as I wear this flesh, but I have maintained optimism, praying, "Help me, God!" very often. Moreover, my best and only remedy to deal with housework is playing praise music. As soon as I turn on the praise music, then my version of party time starts in my kitchen. Likewise, whenever I feel lonely or depressed, I choose to listen to praise. Then, the Holy Spirit lifts me up and charges my battery fully and immediately.

However, entering this season, I noticed something different in my inner world. That is, I felt excited even without good news, since the middle of August 2018, after Mom's sickness. But nothing was going on presently, neither had any vacation plans been made. What I assumed was that there were a bunch of seeds planted as dreams in my heart for the coming years. I have never, in my grown-up life, been so optimistic like this for me and my family's unknown future. Daring to say this, I sensed more closely the plan of God for me. There must be something good for me because I cannot resist this conviction of my heart that I'm moving forward. No, the better saying is, "God is moving me forward!"

Once again, I asked God to advance my life in the last month of 2018. My first big prayer like this was made almost ten years ago, from 2008 to 2011. It was a three years' prayer, and God didn't seem to be answering it at all. In spite of some bitterness and frustration, I had no other choice than to pray. It made me keep crying out to Him, even wetting my pillow, to take me out of my nail salon business and promote my life. I had lived in chains of generational bondage, which I had no understanding of, but I was stuck in the middle, in the long and heavy trial of an immigrant's life—a generation to be sacrificed for the next generation—without any real dream for myself.

Specifically, my prayer at the time was that God would grant me the ability to perceive the beauty of every season of His creation. Simply put, I wanted to sense and enjoy the beautiful changes of nature and breathe them in. The day I heard my friend delighting in the beauty of the season, in the middle of a dark and gloomy winter, I was appalled. Even before winter, I couldn't sense any beauty in the most beautiful autumn season, a season that most people admire. I was starting to recognize that my heart and senses were numb to the aesthetics of my environment; I needed Claritin, figuratively speaking.

Experiencing an unresolved knot with my mysterious husband, a needy mom who depends on me fully and urgently, demanding young children, and my possessive business, I was just trying hard to survive day-to-day. There had been many years already where I had no idea which season I had been in. Since I had been a poor immigrant when I came to America at twenty-one years old, I don't remember any fun in my twenties or thirties—having had to work, raise children and try to make ends meet. And it only grew worse. I thought I could drop dead at any moment in the middle of my work. I felt like I had no life because I had lived without a dream for so long, except for the dream of raising children. I had no idea that I could ask God for anything other than help with finances, kids, and ongoing problems.

It was in the midst of it all—I was hanging on the word of God, my only lifeline—that I started to memorize and recite Scripture. The very first verse I memorized was Proverbs 3:5-6, "Trust in the Lord with all your heart. Lean not on your own understanding. In all ways acknowledge Him then He will straighten your path."

Every time I recited it in my head, I was stuck on the very first line. "Trust in the Lord, with all your heart." "With all your heart" stunned me. *How can I ever do that?* I had no idea. I did not know how. I was so afraid of how much my heart would weigh on God's scale because the status of my heart was changing every day. I could always find worries and doubts in my heart. At that time, I had been only a child spiritually, so weak and naive in every way, far from the "soldier" stage. *So how could I make all my heart trust God totally?*

God raised me slowly from there. During my nail business, for eight years, God taught me, through a spiritual course of intensive discipline, to the next level: "Live not by sight, but by faith" (2 Corinthians 5:7).

Romans 8:38 reads,

For I am convinced that neither death nor life, neither angels nor demons, neither the present nor the future, nor any powers, neither height nor depth, nor anything else in all creation, will be able to separate us from the love of God that is in Christ Jesus our Lord.

This verse above also supported me powerfully in the most depressing season of my life. Besides, the *Breaking Free* Bible study by Beth Moore had seemed to be arranged and prepared just for me for the next tough season. God poured out His unfailing love to saturate and carry me in His arms. He knew exactly what I needed! God advanced my life from there, ending my business, and has changed it radically since then. Before I knew it, I was at a new level of faith, lifting other sisters and praying for others not to give up.

Now, watching the scenery of any given moment brings the purest delight to my heart. Breathing and soaking in the beauty of God's creation have become my privilege from my answered prayer.

Meanwhile, God led me to a massage therapist position from the nail tech job, replacing new desires in my heart and allowing me to work only part-time. Immediately I started to join many different ministries, which I had never had time for before, and it influenced and nurtured me. Last year, one funny thing I realized and told my children was that I was born-again in 2000 but have only recently matured into a spiritual adult.

In the fall of 2018, I sent God my biggest prayer, a prayer concerning my purpose and my future! Years ago, whenever there were prayer meetings, I felt envious of others' prayers. They wanted to know the will of God and be able to do His will! And now I asked God evermore seriously to show His will for my life and expressed that I wanted to live a life pleasing to Him! "Please use me for your glory!"

As time went by, I found myself saying similar prayers, and they went deep and deeper! *How exciting it was!* As my prayers became stronger, my faith became bigger! Furthermore, I perceived more and more things. My thoughts connected like dominos, then toppled and fell into a request for a new direction for my life, which I naively thought was my own idea. I am convinced now that it was God's. He wanted me to ask Him more about what He had planned for me as my loving Father. He said: "You don't receive it because you didn't ask for it" (Matthew 7:7–8).[5]

People around me said that they were sad and depressed that summer was over too soon. I heard nothing but complaints. In contrast, for no known reason, I found myself full of hope and anticipation. I told one

---

5 Joyce Meyer has said it in this way.

of my friends about this unjustifiable yet extraordinary feeling of positivity. Her response was that I am pregnant, pregnant with something great God is going to do! *Woohoo!*

Now I'm determined to wait, well and patiently, keeping this hope and joy. I know that no matter how long it takes, it will fit God's timeline! And even if He doesn't show me anything, then I will still not be disappointed because I believe He knows what's best for me.

> *I remain confident of this: I will see the goodness of the LORD in the land of the living. Wait for the LORD; be strong and take heart and wait for the LORD.*
>
> **Psalm 27:13–14**

> *See, I am doing a new thing! Now it springs up; do you not perceive it? I am making a way in the wilderness and streams in the wasteland.*
>
> **Isaiah 43:19**

> *I will go before you and will level the mountains; I will break down gates of bronze and cut through bars of iron. I will give you hidden treasures, riches stored in secret places, so that you may know that I am the LORD, the God of Israel, who summons you by name.*
>
> **Isaiah 45:2–3**

If you remain in me and my words remain in you, ask whatever you wish, and it will be done for you.

John 15:7

Not only so, but we also glory in our sufferings, because we know that suffering produces perseverance; perseverance, character; and character, hope. And hope does not put us to shame, because God's love has been poured out into our hearts through the Holy Spirit, who has been given to us.

Romans 5:3–5

May the God of hope fill you with all joy and peace as you trust in him, so that you may overflow with hope by the power of the Holy Spirit.

Romans 15:13

For we live by faith, not by sight.

2 Corinthians 5:7

Let us then approach God's throne of grace with confidence, so that we may receive mercy and find grace to help us in our time of need.

Hebrews 4:16

Now faith is confidence in what we hope for and assurance about what we do not see.

Hebrews 11:1

And without faith it is impossible to please God, because anyone who comes to him must believe that he exists and that he rewards those who earnestly seek him.

Hebrews 11:6

3. Divine Appointment (Spring 2019)

Prior to any massage session, a brief consultation with a client about her body condition and how she desires her session to be, etc., is very important. First, I try to keep all the information the client gave me in mind as I start up a massage. I minimize my talking but speak gently to check on her comfort level, adjusting the headrest, bolster, temperature of the bed, and even the volume of music.

Unlike some other service fields, most of the massage clients come with a heavy look, one of fatigue and discomfort. Some even look depressed, drawing my attention irresistibly to them. Sensing more than their physical need, sometimes I open with this: "You are in good hands! Don't worry about anything. Somebody up there is in control! Everything will be fine. Just relax! Imagine that you are in a vacation place, your favorite place! Breathe deeply once more!"

Like most other therapists, I enter meditation with my client, directing breathing control. I like to begin my sessions with a head-to-feet warm-up, a technique I used to massage my grandmother, as a prelude to my massage. Assuring the client peace and comfort is my first job. At the onset of each session, I silently pray for the needs of the client and the will of God, or I pray a personal prayer.

After a couple of minutes of actual massage, I ask the client only about desired pressure and remind her to let me know if anything is bothering her during the session. It is really important to be aware of which part of the body to target and to exert just the right amount of pressure she likes. I try to give each and every person a customized and satisfying massage, remembering their preferences. Even though some clients identify no problem areas, their necks and shoulders are tight anyway, so I always give extra attention there.

Usually, most clients don't like to talk during a session, but they relax. Some sigh, and I must check: "Are you okay?" Others fall asleep and even snore. Then I rest my mind in His presence with prayer while my body performs the massage to the tranquil music. It soothes my soul and spirit, and this is the reason I can do this job currently.

"You are petite, but you are so strong!"

"Oh, thanks. Do you like my pressure?"

"Oh, yes! Very much. Thank you. It's so good."

One client talked to me like that briefly. Then, she said she was stressed about her children. I was startled at that, sensing something else, the Spirit inviting.

In this case, I responded, "Oh, I'm sorry! How many children do you have?"

"Just two. Do you have children?" she asked me back.

"I have two also," I answered briefly.

"How old are they?" she asked me for more.

"They are big. I have two grown-up children. I married young, and I started early," I answered with some laughter.

She said, "Oh yes? Wow, you don't look that old. My children are big too. One is out of college, and one is in college. They are twenty-five and twenty. How old are yours?" she continued.

I responded to her nicely, but I encouraged her to relax, knowing I should not initiate the conversation first as a professional in this field. Then she said she'd *like* to talk. At that, I felt pure delight in my heart. In that case, I could engage. This was a lengthy, eighty-five-minute massage, and she obliged me to talk non-stop. Although she must have had no idea, she allowed and agreed with me to invite the Holy Spirit into our conversation.

As she was asking about my children's ages, which were similar ages to her children's ages, she also asked about my culture and my expectations about their dating partners. Maybe her curiosities stemmed from our shared Asian heritage? She asked an abundance of questions, as one might interview a celebrity.

Wow! She honed in on my target area, the most critical part of my present life, all my favorite topics to talk about as a mom, and she wanted to hear all about it.

If we go back, within the last story of my first chapter, I wrote that my heart was shattered at my daughter's confession about her boyfriend in 2017. Hence, I answered her question directly. "I had instructed, prayed, and asked my children to ensure only one thing about their future dating mates: they had to be believers of Christian faith." I continued, "I'm a born-again Christian, and that means I experienced Jesus and am certain that I am saved by grace, and I will go to heaven." Right after that, I made sure to check on her thoughts. "I'm sorry, I should stop. I want you to relax."

She urged me to go on and tell her more! I said, "Are you sure? I'm not supposed to talk about God and faith while working."

Then she said, "I don't care. I'm interested in your story." It was a divine appointment with her. As we were talking, the air we were breathing filled with sweet aroma. My client and I were delighted with each other.

I told her that I had never known joy until I was born again in the year 2000. Telling her I'm a fatherless child born and raised in the culture of Confucianism, I inquired, "Do you know what that was like?" I answered myself, "I had experienced shame growing up, from my own teachers. I internalized this shame. However, the Bible says I'm not ashamed in Christ Jesus! God Himself says He becomes a Father to the fatherless and talks all about His love for me. How could I not be healed by His non-stop love?"

"Wow!" my client responded with exclamation. I said, "Oh, thank you. You are so kind. Now I want you to enjoy the massage!" Refocusing on massage, at the same time, I prayed to God, *Oh God, thank You! Please make me go on!*

"Surely, I love a story like that. So real! Go on! I'm enjoying your massage too!" She yearned to hear more. Her voice was pleading.

"Do you want to know how I was born-again?"

"Yes!" my client answered passionately.

"I knew Jesus as the Son of God, and He died on the cross for my sins and rose from the grave. Nevertheless, for me to be born-again, I had to acknowledge my sinfulness from being imperfect. Do you know what? My problem until then was that I had thought I was a good person. Yet, there was always somebody who wasn't good before my eyes. But I realized there is only one perfect being. That is God, and in His eyes, we are all the same. There is no better or worse. Even a hateful thought is like murder; that's written in the Bible (1 John 3:15). Sin is sin because God doesn't sin. He doesn't know sin; that's why He is called holy, so holy."

At that, she said "Yes," quietly.

I went on, "Long story short, I simply had to admit my sinfulness from the bottom of my heart to God. I was so afraid to admit it. Right then, a beam of light shone on me, and it was pouring out from the cross! It was an unbelievable experience! Then suddenly, the well of joy in my heart overflowed! That was how I was born-again. It was the biggest turning point of my life! My 'before' and 'after' started right there. The Bible says you will know the truth, and the truth will set you free. I was freed indeed and found true joy. How could it be possible?" I was breathless but quickly added, "Are you okay with this? I can stop now."

"No, I like it," she said calmly.

I have to give her a good massage! It was hard to focus while talking so much.

Then, she asked me, "So are your children dating believers?"

I answered, "No. Not my daughter. My son will, but he doesn't date yet." I told her the following account on the same night that only a year ago my daughter, Ashley, had confessed her relationship with a non-believing boyfriend.

I started with, "I watched my heart shatter into pieces, and I had to go through seasons of valleys, deserts, and oceans. I had prayed to God to take Ashley's boyfriend away from her. I had prayed and prayed to get rid of him, but God never answered my prayers."

"Then, it was last summer when Ashley's boyfriend was sick with a fever for a couple of weeks. One of several test results indicated he had lymphatic cancer. Ashley collapsed at the news and cried devastatingly. I felt worse than terrible. I had never wanted him to be sick like that, even though I was not so thrilled at the idea of him, a non-believer, as my daughter's future spouse."

"The next thing I knew, I was praying for him. God made me pray for him on my knees day and night. I had never imagined that I would pray desperately for him, for his healing, his health, his faith, his salvation, and his blessing to God. Through those prayers, God created something unbelievable for him in my heart, a brand new love. I texted my prayers to him with Scripture verses. He thanked me back."

"All the sisters in my small group and friends prayed for him, and before we knew it, God granted the miracle and healed him. When he had another blood test at a bigger hospital later, it came back clear. There was no evidence of cancer. I could not believe that God answered our prayers that quickly. God showed His pure love for Ashley's boyfriend, and now I was surprised at myself, having full love for him also." So I told my client joyfully, "Now I'm filled with only love for him—my future son-in-law—and they will marry soon."

What I added then amazed me because it was the first time I heard what my mouth had to say, "God exposed my pride and prejudice, which had to be removed, through Ashley's boyfriend. Therefore, it was God's will to bring him to us so that we could show him who God is and how much God loves him through us."

Before finishing the massage, I concluded, "I know one thing clearly: God loves you equally just as much as He loves me. He doesn't love me more. He must be yearning for you because you are the missing one. The Bible says Jesus leaves the ninety-nine behind to find the one who is lost (Matthews 18:12–14). That is why this happened today with you, for His divine appointment. God speaks to you through me right now; He loves you! He also loves your children and family so much!"

After the session, when my client came out of the room, we hugged each other for a long time. She thanked me once more while I genuinely reciprocated her appreciation for listening to me for such a long time. We looked at each other with tearful eyes and shared the love from our hearts.

I never know when the next divine appointment will be. Sometimes even though I pray for the client, sensing her need and yearning for any chance to minister, there is absolutely no clue, and often nothing happens. However, I *have* experienced numerous unbelievable divine appointments arranged by the Holy

Spirit. It always happens when I least expect it. Then, when I find myself already in it, nothing can stop us, and it overwhelms me every time. That is why I want to shout out and share this unexplainable joy that cannot be restrained inside of me thanks to the boundless power of God.

Thank God that He cured and humbled me through Ashley's boyfriend. He showed me that He loves Ashley's boyfriend as much as Ashley (they married in fall 2019. I love my son-in-law God sent!).

Ashley and I are laughing and talking about this in complete comfort. I never imagined I would have a Japanese son-in-law. As a matter of fact, Korea and Japan don't get along historically. Recently the news between them has been the worst. I remembered Corrie ten Boom, who was a victim during World War II and a Dutch evangelist, speaking all about forgiveness and love of God throughout Germany. I pray for a Korean evangelist to tell the Japanese about forgiveness and the love of God!

And afterward, I will pour out my Spirit on all people. Your sons and daughters will prophesy, your old men will dream dreams, your young men will see visions.

Joel 2:28

But whoever loves God is known by God.

1 Corinthians 8:3

My command is this: Love each other as I have loved you.

John 15:12

Whoever does not love does not know God, because God is love.

1 John 4:8

And so we know and rely on the love God has for us. God is love. Whoever lives in love lives in God, and God in them.

1 John 4:16

4. The Trip to Korea (Spring 2019)

Part 1

There is an annual women's conference organized by the Real-Life Women's Group under the Assembly of God in New Jersey. It attracts thousands every February, and I have attended for almost ten years with my friends.

In 2018, the speaker of the conference was Sheila Walsh. Unlike my friends, I didn't know who she was—a famous Christian television host, speaker, and author. She never knew she made me cry that day, immediately after she started her speech. It was a speech about her life-long suffering and missing her father, who died suddenly with an aneurysm when she was only five years old. She spoke about how God delivered her from her affliction. Unexpectedly, she hit home; I missed my own father. Until then, I had been in control. I was content and didn't have issues talking about the fact that I was a fatherless child, even though I missed him at times.

But Sheila's entire speech poked and pressed me. I agonized over my father to the extent that I couldn't bear it anymore. During the conference, I wept and prayed a forgotten prayer about my father, like a little child again, but even more seriously. Finally, I asked God to help me meet my dad if he was still alive.

Waiting until the evening for the proper time to call Korea, the time difference is about twelve hours, seemed so long. I talked to my cousin who had found my father's information back in 2001 and begged her to find him once more for me. I needed to at least know that he was alive. He would be about eighty-five years old now.

In the meantime, I told my husband that we could visit Korea together next year and we could celebrate our thirtieth wedding anniversary with a big trip. I tried to think about it as a dream vacation. It had been twenty-five years since I visited my country, as I hadn't had any desire to go, not like a typical Korean—not like my husband.

After I'd gotten this desire, I called my cousin every week and then every month to check out what she had found out about my father. What she kept telling me wasn't hopeful because policies had changed in Korea. There was a new, special law called the Privacy Act, a personal information protection act. This meant that no one could find anyone unless they were related by law. She told me that she would utilize other routes to find him, so I waited.

If I could not find him, I thought, I would not visit Korea. Aside from seeing him, I didn't have any desire to go on an expensive trip to Korea; I'd rather go on another cruise in the Caribbean. While my husband wants to go to see his mom and family more often—he goes by himself—I don't desire to go there much since my mom is here with me. The last time I visited was back in 1994; even when Mom was there, my husband and I had to travel all around the country to visit with our relatives. It was far from a vacation, and when I came back to the States, I became pretty depressed.

When I left my home city, Mokpo, for Seoul after graduating high school, I never wanted to go back to it. Furthermore, when I left my home country, Korea, I never wanted to return there either. What do I miss?

Nothing. There were no nostalgic memories to cherish; I remember nothing but affliction.

One time, I was going to share my heart with my Korean friend here in America in about 2007. I was on the phone with her and feeling melancholic, saying, "I have a problem. I have no patriotism for Korea like the average Korean. I don't even cheer for them crazily like my husband does when we watch soccer games on TV."

At that, she quickly became angry at me, saying, "That's really wrong. That's not right. Are you not a Korean? Do you think you are an American? No matter how much you try, you can't be like a real American. After all, you are a Korean. You should love your mother country then. I have to go." She hung up on me.

If she had been a little softer toward me at the beginning, showing pity or sympathy, I could have told her everything, even explained my damaged Korean identity. However, most of my Korean friends reacted to me just like that, quickly judging me, although they were all Christians. Anyway, I knew that I couldn't share deeply with them on a cultural level.

Although I was waiting calmly and patiently for God's answer about whether to go or not to go to Korea, trusting that He had given me the desire to miss my father through Sheila Walsh's message, I wouldn't have any answers until November.

Father, please answer this for me! Why do I have to go

to Korea if not to find him? Do You still want me to go or not? Please say no if I should not go at all! I don't want to waste my time and money! Don't I have to spend my money wisely?

Then I thought, if he is deceased, then I won't have to go, so I delayed purchasing airline tickets until my husband started bugging me. It would have been a simple decision for some, but I couldn't make one because I didn't know the will of God clearly about the matter.

Then in late November, I happened to drive into Woodbridge, where we had lived for about five years before moving to our present home. It had been a while since I passed through the area, though it's not too far. Driving on St. George's Ave, I felt a certain friendliness. Every old building I recognized made me grin. The street and the whole atmosphere in town was embracing me sweetly and, at the moment, God spoke to me in my heart: "Are you happy about the old town you lived in for only five years? Then how much happier will you be to see your home city where you grew up? Go! Go and enjoy!"

Oh, Yes! That's right, God! That's it! Thank You! That was the precise answer I needed: God wants me to go to Korea!

I was so happy to hear Him. Whenever He answers, it suits what is needed and becomes perfect. Airline tickets were purchased right away.

Part 2

It was clear that God wanted me to go to Korea, but if I did not find my father, then what for? That would be the real question: why did He make me miss my father suddenly and crazily? That was why I had searched for him throughout the year, but every result was negative. Was I not driven by God?

God made it known in my heart at that moment. I knew what He knew about me, and He knew me so well. Only missing my father could hook me into wanting to go to Korea. There was no other reason for me to go to Korea. He let Sheila Walsh touch my heart so that her words drove me to the decision to go to Korea. God was successful with his plan for me. *So Father, will I meet my earthly biological father then? Can I? Please, God!*

Until I left home in March, I didn't receive any information about my father. However, I was following God's direction to visit Korea and was getting excited about the trip. So I asked friends to pray for me to find my father and also to pray for my heart to be guarded just in case I didn't find him. I didn't want to be disappointed, so I resisted too much hope and kept my peace.

Whatever Your will is, God, I will be satisfied!

It was Saturday when my husband and I arrived

in Korea in March 2019. On Monday, first thing in the morning, I went to the district government building. I was led to an officer who was in charge of a department similar to Human Resources. I had to tell him my bizarre life story of wanting to find my father. Everybody in the office who heard my story looked stunned, but the solution was impossible because I could not prove he was my father or that I was his daughter. The man kindly offered to drive me to the address on the letter I received from my father in 2001, but we found nobody living at that address. He told me to wait until the afternoon while he checked with some people nearby. After a few hours, he called me and said that he had found no clues. I cried out to God for a moment—*Why, God?*—but I knew I had reached the point that I had to give it up. Until I received that last phone call in the afternoon, I was slightly hopeful. It turned out to be nothing, and I couldn't ruin my whole trip. Thank God for guarding my heart so the bad news didn't break it. *God will show his special will for me about this trip!*

"Above all else, guard your heart, for everything you do flows from it" (Proverbs 4:23).

We were in the same city, Pusan, where my in-laws lived. Pusan is really a gorgeous city; almost half of the city features a beautiful beach along the coastline.

My husband and I chose not to tell my in-laws about my journey to find my father so that they would not be troubled. My mother-in-law was aging very gracefully and was nicer to me than ever—she was a little tough at the beginning of my marriage, and I had felt very uncomfortable with her. My other sisters and brothers-in-law were all aging beautifully and blessed us wholeheartedly. In fact, everybody in my husband's family became believers in Christ over the course of their lives, and maybe that was why they all looked more peaceful and content than ever. My husband and I met lots of his relatives and spent an amazing time with them. Every individual seemed respectful and looked precious to me.

Then my husband and I went our separate ways for three days: I visited my old home city, Mokpo, after thirty years, since 1987, because I missed a visit in 1994. As soon as the bus entered the region of Mokpo, my heart started to leap with joy. The whole atmosphere was so different and sweet as if the Holy Spirit set out some welcoming placards all over the city for me. Despite the huge changes, it was surprisingly amicable to me. I never knew it was so beautiful, and if my memory was right, it was impossible to feel that delightful here. My male cousin Ki, who is three years younger than me, who I hadn't seen for over thirty years, was waiting for me at the bus terminal. At a glance, I could recognize him easily. I loved this cousin so much when I was young. He was cute and shy, so he was like my pet whenever he came to Grandmother's, and he was still so adorable and even so humorous, making me laugh the whole time.

Everybody I met there was amazing: my aunt, uncle-in-law—I had prayed for him during the winter for his severe injury, and God was healing him so well—and my cousin Ji and their families were all so sweet and fabulous. I met my next-door friend's big sister. Also, I met my two favorite high school teachers, Mr. Kwon and Mrs. Lee. It was so weird that we didn't feel the gap of time, or maybe it's better to say we could overcome the long absence over time by the mysterious Him, my Father, who was bestowing all the blessings.

Above all, the most unbelievable thing was waiting for me. It happened that there was a transformation of my grandmother's house—along with the next-door neighbor's—into a private nursing home, and the name of it was *love*, "Love Nursing Home." Wow! The signboard, "Love," above the small building stunned me. I stood there in awe of it for some minutes. As I started to take some pictures, I saw something famil-iar behind it. When I went closer, I couldn't believe my eyes. It was that old mud-stone wall between my grandmother's and the Catholic Church. The wall was over fifty years old, probably the age of the Catholic church. I have no idea of its true age, but it stood time-lessly to me.

It was standing there like a symbol and a witness to the girl who had spent her early years here and had come back thirty years later completely transformed. The memory of it didn't hurt me but soothed me be-yond description as if it were telling me: "I had seen all of you. You were never alone! Welcome! I'm proud of you!" The nurturing voice echoed in my soul.

It was a moment of proof, revealing the truth that God had never left me even when I was young, even when I could not hear, and even when I doubted Him. Suddenly I was thinking, *Was this God who preserved this wall from being destroyed to show it to me and welcome me?* This thought of happiness showered me.

Walking up and down the slope, I was surprised that it wasn't as far to go up and down as I had remembered. For the child climbing up and down all those years, it seemed so big. At the bottom of the slope, the intersection was small and narrow, but it was very busy and huge for me as a child. To my surprise, there were a few of the same stores and a pharmacy I had to run to for Grandmother. It was just refreshing and friendly to look around my old home city, with no hint of any pain from the past.

On Saturday morning, when I was leaving Mokpo, I got in a cab to go to the train station to go to Seoul. Through the window of the cab, I was taking some pictures of the scenery. The cab driver was asking me if I was traveling, so I told him I was from the United States and was visiting Mokpo, my birthplace. Then I asked him if Mokpo was his hometown, and he said it was not.

He said he was from a small island near Mokpo harbor, but he didn't visit it for a quarter-century since he had a painful memory of it. The second he said that, I knew we were entering a divine appointment. For the next ten minutes, I told him about my shameful identity and that I never wanted to come back to this country nor to my old home city because of the painful memory.

But God saved me through my Savior, God's Son Jesus, who died for my sins and who rose from the grave. That was how I became set free from all the shame this country had thrown at me because the truth you receive sets you free. So I am not the same person I used to be but became a new creation, and the same God who loves me unconditionally wants me to tell him how God loves him as a missing child. It was only about ten minutes until I arrived at the train station, but that was enough, and I was able to tell him about the non-stop love of God.

My husband was coming from Pusan, and I arrived in Seoul earlier on Saturday. In metropolitan Seoul, I planned to go to a particular church the next day on Sunday for the Lord's day. It was very important to me to go for the service at this particular church; God showed me from the U.S. Until then, it was a perfect trip with only a pleasant spirit.

When I arrived at the train station in Seoul, a relative who wanted to see me met me, and we had lunch together. However, after I met him, I started to have a sudden severe headache, and I found myself depressed, with no strength all of a sudden, canceling other plans. Then I was thinking, *Will I be able to go to church tomorrow?* Immediately I had to pray. Then I knew it was the enemy who became so jealous of me and my trip, especially for the hidden purpose of it. My relative didn't know it, but the enemy came with him. So during lunch with him, it was the enemy which stressed me. This relative who wasn't a believer expressed disgust at my faith in Jesus, but he was so proud and concerned, at the same time, about his wealth and success. What challenged me was that I was going to meet him again the next day at his home after the service as scheduled.

Just then, my husband arrived from Pusan, showing up at our hotel room very sick. He went straight to bed without dinner. It was Saturday evening, and I had to check out a couple of local pharmacies around the hotel, but they were closed. He was sick with a fever overnight, and there was nothing I could do but pray.

All I could do was pray and wait. I knew what the enemy was trying to do, intimidate and discourage me. So I was determined not to give in to him. I wasn't intimidated or discouraged, but instead, I trusted God.

God was so faithful, and my husband was better towards dawn. It was just a one-day flu. So he felt fine with no fever and let me go to church that morning.

Even finding that church was dramatic in the extremely busy and crowded metropolitan city. I don't know which is more complicated: New York City or Seoul. After over an hour in subways, changing lines twice, and asking people for help, I arrived at my stop. As I was exiting the subway toward the street, I had to ask a passerby the direction to this church. The person said he didn't know, but someone who was running past heard me say the church name and called out, "Follow me!" He was an angel sent by God to get me to a shuttle that would take me to the church. It was merely a five-minute walk to the shuttle, but it was in a bustling area where I never could have found it for myself.

The sermon was the perfect message from God: how to love my relatives. God gave the perfect reminder and fuel for me: serve them just the way you want to serve God (Colossians 3:22–4:1).

My husband and I spent some time alone shopping. Then we visited many people together for the rest of the trip. We visited my uncle, aunts, cousins, nephews, a niece, his nephew, and our friends — a group of precious college friends. I even met my next-door neighbor from my hometown.

Every individual was so precious. They gave me so much delight, and it filled my heart. I never knew how much I could enjoy all these lovely people, regardless that many of them didn't know Jesus yet.

The whole trip to Korea was smooth sailing except

that one attack by the enemy and some traffic jams. Our twelve days had passed like clouds in a breezy sky, and now my husband and I were at the airport to come back to America, my home, where my citizenship is. It was about time to come back home, and I was slightly missing it. Thank God for my mom being well and my children taking good care of their grandmother. Everything and everyone made this trip possible. It was time to go home.

But suddenly, I found myself missing this country already when I hadn't even left yet. As I was standing in a line to board the plane, I had that same sad feeling as when I had to send my daughter to a different country, away from the U.S.

Why do I feel so sad? Why do I miss all these people I don't know?

My eyes were busily absorbing all the scenes and people around me. As I looked around, the atmosphere of this mother country, revisited after twenty-five years, was intense to me, as if it were missing me already, sending its daughter away.

Until that moment, I had never realized this country could be *my* mother country. I possessed a hidden love for this country. And Korea, she embraced me as her own. It caused me to burst into tears, which surprised my husband. He shook his head in amazement. And it was a totally unexpected thing for me as well.

Overall, it was a great trip to my motherland, Korea, but I still didn't have the answer as to why the trip was mandatory when I couldn't find my father. For a couple of months, I had to process what God meant for me with this trip, and the answer appeared.

My God, who knows me so well, had to bring me to Korea by prodding my heart to miss my father at first.

It was only for one purpose, God's purpose. He arranged steps for me to take toward His purpose. I had to go to Korea to recover and restore my love for the country. He was preparing me for something in the future. Before arriving at His plan for the future, I was supposed to be full of love for this land and these people. Otherwise, I would be nothing and of no use for the ultimate purpose He has for me. *Whatever He does, He does it so perfectly!*

Once in a while, I get to wonder about one thing over and over. *Why does the Almighty God, who created heaven and earth, and the universe, love me so much? How can God take care of everyone on Earth, over seven billion people, individually, yet care for me so intimately?*

If anyone asks me for one word to describe God, it's faithful. He is a faithful God. He keeps His promises. My God is a God of promises (Hebrews 6:13–14).

This trip to Korea was a special event designed to confirm God's faithfulness to me and my life from the past, through my present, to the future. This trip was a confirmation.

And there is one more unbelievable thing He has done through the trip. He has decorated the ending of my book with His prepared and given story! My life story tells how He has loved me with His non-stop love!

I can't give Him enough, but I still give Him my praise, honor, and glory forever to eternity! "I love You, my God, Jesus, more than ever! You satisfy me!"

Suppose one of you has a hundred sheep and loses one of them. Doesn't he leave the nine-ty-nine in the open country and go after the lost sheep until he finds it?

Luke 15:4

Then you will know the truth, and the truth will set you free.

John 8:32

If I speak in the tongues of men or of angels, but do not have love, I am only a resounding gong or a clanging cymbal. If I have the gift of prophecy and can fathom all mysteries and all knowledge, and if I have a faith that can move mountains, but do not have love, I am nothing. If I give all I possess to the poor and give over my body to hardship that I may boast, but do not have love, I gain nothing.

1 Corinthians 13:1–3

And now these three remain: faith, hope and love. But the greatest of these is love.
1 Corinthians 13:13

He who did not spare his own Son, but gave him up for us all—how will he not also, along with him, graciously give us all things?
Romans 8:32

This is how God showed his love among us: He sent his one and only Son into the world that we might live through him.
1 John 4:9

When God made his promise to Abraham, since there was no one greater for him to swear by, he swore by himself, saying, " I will surely bless you and give you many descendants."
Hebrews 6:13–14

5. How He Encourages Me

The First Episode (this episode happened about ten years ago and makes me grin whenever I remember it)

It was my day off, around noon, at the beginning of July when I stopped by a local Walmart. As I walked in, my eyes were wide and busy scanning the many random products on display. Then suddenly, I was surprised to find something my husband had wished for (though, currently, I cannot recall what it was). Since online shopping wasn't as advanced as it is now, I had been searching in stores for this particular product for my husband, to no avail. Yet, there at Walmart, I found it so easily. So excited to find it without effort, I had to call my husband to let him know. One thing I totally forgot was that it was usually very busy at my husband's company in the morning until midday. After a few rings, my husband answered with a rough low voice, "Why?" But I was still joyful to tell him what I just found. The next second, my ear and my whole head were hurt by his thunderous yelling, "Do you think I care for it?" and he hung up on me at once.

With such a mean telling off by my husband, I couldn't help but feel like I was being bombed in the middle of the open area in Walmart. Nobody heard how he scolded me loudly over the phone, but I was blushed and humiliated as if everyone heard him. Comforting myself, *That is nothing. I don't care. It's all right!* I looked for things I needed busily. Suddenly, the sign of McDonald's caught my eyes as I was paying at the cash register. Although I don't usually go to McDonald's by myself without children, I felt hungry, and I must have needed something to comfort me.

A tear dropped from my eye and rolled over my cheek as I bit a burger sitting in McDonald's. I tried to think positive thoughts. I wiped my tears stealthily at the embarrassment of myself — sitting facing Walmart with no wall to hide my visible sorrow. I wished there was no one who knew me there to see me like this. As soon as I wiped my tears and bit my burger again, a random child pushed his face right in front of my nose and said, "Hi!" with a smile.

I almost had a heart attack but mustered a "Hi!" back to him. He had already run away from me.

Thank God he didn't see my tears! It was definitely after I wiped my tears and sighed a big sigh. I couldn't tell who he was at all at the moment, but then I was able to remember him, one of my fourth-graders at Vacation Bible School, which had been held only last week at our church.

It was a very successful Vacation Bible School, but I still couldn't remember his name; there were nearly thirty students in my class. I was astonished that he could identify me that easily among the crowd, in a new environment where I must have looked like a completely different person, with different clothes and a different hairstyle, even while eating a burger.

Now intending to thank him for recognizing and greeting me, I looked for him where he was sitting inside McDonald's. He was sitting farthest from me with a woman, maybe his mom. So before leaving McDonald's, I walked over to him to initiate conversation as his former Vacation Bible School teacher. Smiling, I asked, "Hi! Have you been reading your Bible?"

At my question, he nodded with a confident smile while eating his burger. I felt pleased with his self-assured answer, so I continued to say, "Wow! I'm so proud of you! Hope you continue to do it! It will give you lots of wisdom! And I want to tell you this to remember! God loves you. All. The. Time!" I emphasized every single word to him. Then I had to ask his name, "By the way, what was your name?"

He said, "Angel." At that, I felt blown away. It wasn't because I heard the name for the first time. Now, I remembered his name. The reason why I felt shocked was that I realized meeting him there wasn't an accident, but an act of God, intending to surprise me.

Walking down toward the parking lot, the last sentence I told him was echoing back for me in my head loudly. "Remember that God loves you. All. The. Time!"

Did God really send the boy to me so I would share with him a message intended also for me? Did He know I would need it? Did He choose the boy named Angel purposefully? When I heard his name, Angel, I knew truly he was sent as God's messenger for me. God surprised me with His witty message to my heart, which was not to forget that He loves me unconditionally.

Sensing His humor, I had to laugh wildly, walking toward my car like a lunatic in the middle of a hot sunny day. As soon as I got in my car, my phone rang. It was my husband. He apologized for his abrupt nastiness before. He tried to explain that at the time I called, it had been the perfect storm, a high-stakes, chaotic situation within his company and *me* on the phone. I could accept his apology gladly because God had comforted me with an event!

Later that day, my children found a bag of leftovers from McDonald's at home and reacted shockingly, asking, "Mom, did you go to McDonald's without us?" I told my children, laughing about how God surprised me with the special message through an angel at McDonald's that day. I've boasted with this episode of how intimately and humorously my God comes to me and to many of my friends, from time to time, just like a child.

The Second Episode (this episode happened in February 2020)

During Sunday worship service, a sudden thought that I must fast today came to me, which wasn't my plan at all until that very moment. So I received it thinking that the Holy Spirit must be guiding me. I was determined to follow it.

There was something that I couldn't shake, no matter how hard I tried not to think about it. It was one email from the Korean publisher about their direction for the manuscript I had sent. It takes a whole month to hear back from them, and that itself consumed me even without labor.

However, at daybreak, the moment I opened my eyes, an email notification from the Korean publisher appeared on my phone's lock screen. The email contained an odd rejection to my manuscript, and this was happening the second time for the same type of rejection.

I noticed my heart didn't sink or break at that, but calmly I thought, *Thank God!* It was then that I perceived it was the Holy Spirit who had cared for me and guarded my heart through fasting. I had fasted the day before. Unbeknownst to me, I was fasting against the rejection I was about to receive. I had anticipated an acceptance without a doubt, just trusting God fully. My humble heart, humbled from fasting, didn't become disappointed with the rejection, no matter how confidently I had been anticipating acceptance.

Despite the fact that I wasn't disappointed with the news, I prayed desperately as I was driving to a Jewish assisted living home where I worked on Monday mornings. "Father, thank You for taking good care of me! I'm all right! The news didn't upset me. Thank You for guarding my heart! I know You are working for me. I trust You to lead me to the right path! I'll leave it to You! Please help me so that I can wait for it better! Please help me to wait well for Your time! But God, can You encourage me? I need it! Please lift me up so that my heart can be full of joy!"

The Jewish assisted living home I worked at on

Monday mornings was the best facility among several facilities for the elders I had visited. However, I couldn't help but feel sad each time I visited there.

The nursing home I go to monthly for our church ministry is located near the Jewish facility, but it has a much better atmosphere. It is open wide, religiously, to all visitors and volunteers, so we were welcomed and often encouraged to lead a good number of elders to salvation there. It was like reaping a harvest each time we visited.

The elders who received Jesus as their Savior on the spot, by the amen of our prayers, were immediately transformed. Their faces, which were gloomy and full of doubt only minutes before, displayed unbelievable smiles. We witnessed how God answered and used us in awe. The elders blessed us back tremendously and much more than we anticipated each time.

This new Jewish assisted living home I visited on Mondays was the complete opposite of the nursing home I just described, the one I visited monthly. They believed only in Judaism, not allowing room for our Savior. That was why I would feel sad when I sensed how God felt about them. Although I'm an evangelist and look for an opportunity to share the gospel at any given chance, it was not easy there since I was hired as a massage therapist, only for a couple of hours on Mondays. Yet, I believed I was carrying out God's will, so I loved the residents with my massage, as the Holy

Spirit led me.

On that particular Monday morning, the day of my rejection email, I felt a little sadder as I watched the residents who didn't know Jesus there, regardless of how beautiful they looked. Maybe it was because of the email I had received in the morning, after all that waiting.

Especially when I massaged Lady Fran, the wave of thoughts I had about her was drowning me. She was calm and kind as usual, but her condition of dementia was worse than anybody's at the place, and she introduced herself each time she saw me. When I met her for the first time, she said, "I have never received a massage here since I came here. My name is Fran. What's your name?" and she kept asking my name, introducing herself to me again and again, every one to two minutes. It had been the same way every time I gave her a massage. So during about ten minutes of massage, we would have introduced ourselves to each other several times.

Thus, I prayed to God in my heart, "Father, even if I was given an opportunity to share with Fran about the gospel, how could I ever be able to do it? Since her dementia is so bad, how will she listen to me and understand it? It's impossible for her. I can't even try it for her at all." Each time when I had her, the same prayer was repeated in me.

Strangely, this Monday, I moved to her front side

after I massaged her shoulder a little from behind. I didn't think or plan anything about it, but before I knew it, I had knelt down on the floor facing her and started to massage her hands. My eyes were looking at her, still not thinking, and my mouth started to talk to her like this with a warm smile. "Fran, you look so beautiful. You look good at your age. I think you are beautiful inside and out." Without thinking much, that certainly came right from my heart.

"Oh, thank you!" She answered me happily.

"Do you know this? I believe in the same God you believe! The God who Abraham, Isaac, and Jacob believed!" At this, Fran smiled even brighter at me. "However, Fran, I know that I will go to heaven sometime later in my life. Do you know that you will go to heaven too?"

"I don't know. I wish I could go there too!" She was still smiling when she answered this!

"I needed my Savior to resolve my sins to go to heaven!" Then Fran's face darkened immediately. "Sins? Do I have sins, too?"

"Surely! You know Adam and Eve sinned against God. That's why we were born with sin originally. And we are not perfect, but sin over and over, unfortunately. That's why we need our Savior!"

Fran seemed to understand this, still looking at me

straight and seriously and nodding at me.

"Fran, you will be sure to go to heaven just like me. I know my Savior, and because of Him, I know I go to heaven! You need your Savior too!"

"A Savior? Who is he?"

"He is Jesus! Yeshua!"

"Oh, but…I'm Jewish…" she frowned her face as she dropped the conversation.

"It doesn't matter; I'm Korean! My ancestors didn't even believe in one God; they were polytheistic. I'm only a Gentile, but I was still saved by Jesus!" She was looking at me, afraid.

"It's so simple! If you believe that Jesus is the Son of God—that He carried your sin, died on the cross, and rose again, you will be saved! If you believe it in your heart and say it with your mouth, then you will be saved! That is written in the Bible!" I shared the news with great excitement and joy, still grabbing her hands!

She looked perplexed, even scared, but her eyes were staring at me! I couldn't believe the whole situation. She was concentrating fully on me! Fran and I were surrounded by the unexplainable power of the Holy Spirit, which was leading us through this special time!

"I, a Korean, was saved among Gentiles because of Jesus! But you are a descendant of Abraham, the Jew, God's people! Shall we pray? Saying that you believe in Jesus?" Still, I couldn't believe she was concentrating on me, and my heart was bursting with joy to see her nodding at me like an innocent child.

"I'm a sinner. I believe that Jesus is the Son of God. And I believe that He died on the cross for my sin and rose again! I believe Jesus is my Savior! Thank You, Jesus. I pray in the name of Jesus! Amen."

I made it as short as possible! She repeated everything after me and said amen with me. Fran was saved by the name of Jesus! Hallelujah!

We both were amazed as we locked eyes and said, "Amen!" This was a miracle! Right away, I remembered Psalm 23 as the Holy Spirit led me, the most popular Psalm she might know, so I started to recite it. Then her voice and soul were even more delighted to recognize it. Then, we recited it together in one voice! As we finished it, we hugged each other excitedly. The joy between us was overwhelming, and I had to recite the same verse once again as our spirits quietly agreed with each other, so she followed me eagerly now, even more confidently. The last verse, "We will dwell in the house of the Lord forever and ever," made us hug again with overflowing joy, almost jumping.

On that Monday, Fran and I spent more than twenty minutes together, even though I lost a sense of time. The nurse who usually arranges my massage time perfectly for the residents was off schedule that day because the Holy Spirit, who makes no mistakes, had planned this long before and advanced it thoroughly so that the time would be secured and prolonged that nobody would come near and bother us, shielding us completely. And how could Fran concentrate on me for twenty minutes! That was the first and the last time that she could do that with me. Surely God broke my misconception of the impossible and performed a miracle right in front of my eyes!

I was speechless and breathless at what God just did for me when I prayed for Him to lift me up and fill my heart with joy. He did it in the same fashion that He separated the sea with two walls, opened the eyes of the blind, and opened the ears of the deaf! He used me to save the patient with the worst condition of dementia! What could comfort me more?

My God loves and takes care of me so intimately in detail, and He never forgets how to fill me up with joy when I need it — to the degree my lungs can't bear any more. So with overblown joy in my lungs and heart, how can I keep this inside and not tell everyone? It doesn't matter if people think I'm overzealous or crazy. I'm consumed by His love, indeed, for His non-stop love!

Remain in me, as I also remain in you. No branch can bear fruit by itself; it must remain in the vine. Neither can you bear fruit unless you remain in me.

John 15:4

Do not conform to the pattern of this world, but be transformed by the renewing of your mind. Then you will be able to test and approve what God's will is—his good, pleasing and perfect will.

Romans 12:2

And we all, who with unveiled faces contemplate the Lord's glory, are being transformed into his image with ever-increasing glory, which comes from the Lord, who is the Spirit.

2 Corinthians 3:18

In all this you greatly rejoice, though now for a little while you may have had to suffer grief in all kinds of trials. These have come so that the proven genuineness of your faith—of greater worth than gold, which perishes even though refined by fire—may result in praise, glory and honor when Jesus Christ is revealed.

1 Peter 1:6–7

Since you have kept my command to endure patiently, I will also keep you from the hour of trial that is going to come on the whole world to test the inhabitants of the earth.

Revelation 3:10

Those whom I love I rebuke and discipline. So be earnest and repent. Here I am! I stand at the door and knock. If anyone hears my voice and opens the door, I will come in and eat with that person, and they with me.

Revelation 3:19–20

Afterword

The Beautiful Thing

When I heard about the Annual Fast starting the next day on Monday, January 4, at church this year, I didn't feel happy. I had completely forgotten about it, even though I've participated every year for the last decade. I considered skipping it this year, but I resisted the thought and decided to do a Daniel fast—no meat, dairy, or sweets—for the next twenty-one days, for my overflowing prayer requests for the new year. *How can I go through everything without God's extra blessings?*

It wasn't as hard as I thought it would be, but I was counting down the final days. Right after I started, the first proof I had waited for came from my publisher. It was delightful but extremely challenging with my level of ability with the English language, even though I had marvelous support from my daughter, Ashley, and Roxanne, my teacher friend.

By the time the last day of fasting approached, I had a weird thought that twenty-one days weren't enough. *Don't I need to do more? Forty days?*

I struggled with the strange desire but felt encouraged, and so I was determined to extend my fast to forty days. Then I felt excited about how God would prevail and grant many favors for me and my family.

On the last day of January, a snowstorm came as forecasted. It was Sunday, and the scenery of white snow on the way back home from church was beautiful. The blizzard shut everything down, but I was filled with exuberance since I was able to send my proof back to my publisher that day.

The next day, on February 1, New Jersey was as white as snow again, and no cars ran on the roads. People didn't seem to mind and just accepted it as another event during the pandemic and stayed home quietly.

My mom and I had an ordinary but comfortable day. We both stayed up late until almost midnight, and I said good night to her and went to my room.

The next day, February 2, my workplace was closed, and my son was working from home upstairs in his room. My husband went to work to check on things at his company. I peeked into my mom's room when I woke up, and she looked sound asleep at 8 a.m. Since she was asleep, I quietly cooked her morning meal and did an extra-long devotion on Romans chapter 12. It was peaceful.

I peeked into my mom's room once more, and she was still sound asleep. She rarely sleeps well, so it was good for her to sleep more. But when I looked at the clock, it was almost noon. It was a good time to wake her up.

I approached her bed and sat down next to her to

wake her, but she looked so asleep and didn't respond. Then I had a chill and started shouting and shaking her. But with no response, I jumped off and cried out to my son Richard. My heart burst, and I wailed on the floor loudly for hours. I've been devastated before, but I felt like I had never felt this way before in my life. Although my mom had lived with oxygen tubes and a BiPAP machine at night for the past two and a half years, she was not bedridden and able to move around. We talked the night before, and I prepared her night snack then too, and I never could have imagined that I wouldn't be able to see her the next morning. After living with us for twenty-two years, my mom was gone so suddenly, without saying goodbye.

**

Gradually, I started putting together the pieces of how God orchestrated my mom's departure throughout the week. First of all, I knew she went to heaven with Jesus. That was an assurance that gave me peace. I knew Mom loved the Lord and loved the word of God, meditating on it day and night. He was her only hope and refuge. And the Lord loved Mom through us. Often, I felt too small to contain all of the love the Lord poured into me for her. And I wasn't as good as I was supposed to be. I failed so much!

I also found my mom's night snack was eaten, and the hot water in her thermostat was almost gone. That meant she was alright until around dawn. She passed peacefully in her sleep. God granted her prayer, which had been her last prayer to God, as she told me that's what she was praying for.

And lastly, looking back, I remembered there had been something different about her the last week. It felt like she surrendered all of her burdens to God. How do I know? At the beginning of the last week, Mom wanted to talk about her past again. She watched my facial expressions carefully, knowing that I was tired of hearing it. I suffered to see her bound by her past pain, repeating it over and over, so she said that it would be the last time. I almost laughed, but told her gently, "Okay, Mom! You can tell me. If you really want to, tell me everything, don't leave anything out. However, this will be the purpose of it. To say it and take it out of your heart, and to give it all to God. Please do not take them back, but let them go. Send them away to God and be set free! So say everything."

Mom started with things I already mostly knew, but she also told me some things that she had never said before, including some secrets about Grandma that only she had known. Sometimes she asked me what if God was mad at her about some things. I was able to assure her that it wasn't her fault and not to worry.

As she talked, I didn't feel any stress or anxiety. I felt strangely comfortable listening to her throughout the week. Yes, she continued her story every day for about a half-hour or more, like a TV drama series, saying each time, "I'm sorry, here's a little more." I was never upset, and I encouraged her to talk more and to let go of everything!

A few days after my mom's passing, I realized the reason I was able to listen to her so well was because there was no anguish or bitterness in her voice. Everything she recalled was just like a story that she told in her calmest voice, which had never happened before. She truly let everything go and surrendered to God. And God received everything and passed her! How beautiful it was!

I probably won't recognize Mom when I go to heaven and see her again because she will be in her best shape! There are no fear, pain, or tears in heaven. I miss you, Mom! I will not cry but be happy! I know Mom wants me to be happy just as God wants me to be. We will see our loved ones again and forever. Most of all, I will see my Savior Jesus and enter His glory. Oh, I can't fathom the beauty of the scene! Thank You, my Lord and Savior Jesus! I love You, Jesus!

In Christ,

Michelle S. Kim

August 2021.

My mom and I lived together for twenty-two years in America.

I honor my mom for her life and the story she has given me for this book.

I love her and will miss her until I see her again in heaven.

Keuija Park passed away to be with the Lord Jesus, on February 2, 2021, during this book's publication. The Lord granted her last prayer to go peacefully in her sleep.

I know Mom loved the Lord and how the Lord loved her so much through me and my children. I often felt too small to contain all the love the Lord wanted to give Mom.

*One thing I ask from the L*ORD*, this only do I seek: that I may dwell in the house of the L*ORD *all the days of my life, to gaze on the beauty of the L*ORD *and to seek him in his temple.*
Psalm 27:4

About the Author

Michelle S. Kim was born and raised in Korea and came to America with her husband in 1989. As an immigrant, she's worked as a nail technician and massage therapist since coming to America, which was a little far from her dreams growing up. She didn't know that she had to live life first and write later, but publishing her book made her dream come true.

Michelle S. Kim is a novice author, with her first book, *Non-Stop Love*, which was also translated and published in Korea in 2020. She has started to lead a Bible study with *Non-Stop Love Study Guide*. She and her family have been living in New Jersey. She has two grown-up children. Visit her website at *non-stoplove.com*.

(Title of the Korean version of this book: 수치범벅에서 기쁨범벅으로 2020)

The mud-stone wall at my grandmother's from the trip to Korea in 2019

9 781637 699362